Dec 13, 2018

For Brett & Sam,

May you always have love and
adventure in your life!

Chasing Dawn

AN ADVENTURE
OF THREE FATHERS
AND FOUR TEENAGERS
BICYCLING
ACROSS AMERICA

PRAISE FOR CHASING DAWN

"Riding your bicycle across America is something every cyclist dreams of doing. It's a classic. A monument. But completing this feat with your kids is something very special indeed. In an era when so many of us live behind screens and in chairs, experience is our most valuable currency. While few of us will realize the dream of riding a bike across the country, Hobbit's gorgeous photos and Shawn's rich storytelling will make you feel as if you lived it."

—Michael Stefanakos, Freeport, Maine

Founder, Southern Maine Mountain Bike Syndicate

"*Chasing Dawn* is an epic journey by a master storyteller, but the deeper story is the gift these families gave to their kids. In a world moving way too fast, these dads did the impossible. They slowed time and shared an experience of a lifetime with their kids. The vision, purpose, and courage that made this trip happen and kept it going across this vast country should awaken in each of us our own adventure, our own trip, and our own gift to give."

—Kelly Wieber, Portland, Oregon

"The moment I felt sadness about the end of their journey was the moment I realized I was on the adventure with them all along. *Chasing Dawn* is a tale of family, friendship, love and the human spirit. And it doesn't stop there. Within these pages is a love of country, a respect for its terrain, and a longing to connect—with the surroundings and with each other. Their adventure invites the reader to join a personal journey and somehow, through the many miles and states, the story transcends the pages and invites the reader to participate."

—Rachel Behrle, Annapolis, Maryland

"Rarely do we take the opportunity to push ourselves so far out of our comfort zone as this adventure must have done for the intrepid travelers. A big, audacious goal broken down into strategic chunks that tested their resilience, persistence, and patience. Utmost admiration for the team on this journey every day made me (almost) want to ride across our much narrower country of New Zealand. Lessons in self, life, and perseverance abound in *Chasing Dawn*."

—Kath Greenhough, Wellington, New Zealand

"More than the miles, Shawn shares the connection of family, friendship, and our great country. The travels of the group show how these tie together through their many trials, which are at times grueling, hilarious, and ultimately transcendent. *Chasing Dawn* is at once a lesson on how great things can be achieved, and a celebration of a simpler life."

—Maura Thornton, Yarmouth, Maine

"What a gift Shawn and his traveling companions gave us in sharing their biking journey from coast to coast. I can vividly imagine their days through the narrative they shared while on the road. The struggles, the wonderful interactions with so many people, the group dynamics, and the growth of each member of the group was phenomenal to experience. I'm so grateful their authentic story is now being shared with the world in *Chasing Dawn*."

—Marion van Leeuwen-Kemmere, the Netherlands

Jim Sayer and daughter Lucy at Dauphin Island, Alabama, along Adventure Cycling's Southern Tier route

FOREWORD

Jim Sayer

> *'Tis the gift to be simple*
> *'Tis the gift to be free*
> *'Tis the gift to be cycling*
> *With your closest family*

One of the many joys of bicycle travel is the occasional opportunity to defy social norms—which can include composing songs in your head while you're riding along, and then belting them out in the middle of nowhere, or sometimes in the middle of a strange town, to the awe and consternation of local residents.

So it happened that I transformed the Shaker song "Simple Gifts," made famous by Aaron Copland, into an ode to my wife and three daughters while riding down the Pacific Coast from Canada to Mexico in the Summer of 2010. I sang it somewhere on the California coast and sang it many times after that, most recently on a 3,100-mile ride with my 18-year-old daughter, Lucy. We journeyed across Adventure Cycling's Southern Tier route, which runs from San Diego, California, to St Augustine, Florida.

That journey with Lucy knitted together so many wonderful people, from my Mom (whose 80th birthday we celebrated at the start) to my Dad (who lives near Austin, TX) to the dozens of friends and strangers who so kindly helped us as we cycled 3,100 miles from Pacific to Atlantic.

Bicycle travel, family, and community fit together so beautifully. It's a gift I've realized from riding with my family all over North America, and the gift so lyrically expressed in *Chasing Dawn*. Shawn and jon have perfectly captured the humor, hardship, and triumph of fathers and their children, making their way across our magnificent, rugged country while navigating the emotions and craziness that come with any arduous adventure.

At the end of the book, Shawn rightly points to how many people regret not pursuing adventures they dream of. Often times, I hear people lament how they wish they could spend, or could have spent, more "quality time" with family members. I'm reminded of one of my favorite quotes from the poet Mary Oliver, "Tell me, what is it you plan to do with your one wild and precious life?"

In that spirit, I hope you'll read *Chasing Dawn*, savor it, and then act. The gift of adventure awaits you, your family, and your friends.

Jim Sayer
Executive Director
Adventure Cycling Association
Missoula, Montana

September 2018

Adventure Cycling Association

Adventure Cycling Association's mission is to inspire, empower, and connect people to travel by bicycle.

Established in 1973 as Bikecentennial, Adventure Cycling is the premier bicycle-travel organization in North America with more than 40 years of experience and 53,000 members.

Learn more at adventurecycling.org.

Jim and his family during their Pacific Coast quest, overlooking Monterey Bay

ISBN-13: 978-0692171448

Permission to use material contact:

G. Shawn Hunter, Words | www.shawnhunter.com
jon o. holloway, Photography and Images | www.jonholloway.com
Abigail Brockelbank, Illustrations | abbibrock@gmail.com
Pam Owen, Editor | nighthawkcomm@gmail.com
Jenn Bulmer, Layout Editor | www.greatmemories.ca
Keith Gordon, Copy Editor

Published by Hunter Group, LLC
24 Woodland Drive, Yarmouth, Maine 04096

Printed in South Korea through Four Colour Print Group, Louisville, Kentucky

TABLE OF CONTENTS

IN THE BEGINNING...

In the late hours of an otherwise forgotten day in 2015, Hobbit called me.
"Hunter, let's do it again."

"Do what again?"

"Ride across country."

"But we never actually rode across the country. We started in Colorado and went east."

"You know what I mean."

"You mean ride across the country."

"Yeah, and we're taking our kids."

"Wait, what? Right. Let's keep talking."

We hung up, but the thought nagged at me.

One sunny day, months later, out for a ride somewhere in rural Maine, I mentioned it to Erich, another friend. He said he needed to think about it.

In 1923, George Mallory was asked why he continually attempted to climb Mt. Everest. "Because it's there" was his famous reply.

One of the primary reasons we took the trip was to seek adventure—to embrace the unknown, to set out to experience new parts of the country, and to encounter new people. But another big reason was that we wanted to give our kids an opportunity to further their development toward adulthood.

Angst, uncertainty, and hostility fill the news these days. Teen bullying and depression are at an all-time high in the United States. We are bombarded daily, even hourly, with news about what's wrong with the world. But despite all that, we wanted to show our kids, and ourselves, what's *right* with the world. We wanted to give them the challenge of

MT. EVEREST BEATS MALLORY:
Mallory disappeared on his third attempt to climb Everest, along with his climbing partner. The bodies were found later, with the question of whether or not they made it to the top still unanswered.

exploration. But most importantly, we wanted to show them how valuable it is to meet people who may be very different, yet with whom they can still connect and understand.

Our thought was that, if we want our kids to possess humility, perseverance, wonder, awe, problem-solving, and gratitude, then we should create an adventure that requires us to persevere through something difficult, solve real problems on the road, and be filled with awe and wonder and splendid sights. And we should accomplish this by ourselves, in unfamiliar—and often challenging—parts of the country, far from help.

THE CREW

Shawn Hunter: I write books, operate a business dedicated to improving company cultures, coach youth soccer, and live in Maine with my wife, Amy, and our three kids. Cycling has been a big part of our lives for a long time. For 10 years, we have been cycling in the *Trek Across Maine* event with our kids. Thousands of people embark on this fun, three-day cycling event to raise money for lung cancer. It's a great and worthwhile endeavor, but in terms of the cycling involved, it's nothing at all like riding across the United States.

Charlie Hunter: Charlie is our eldest son. At 16, he is tall, and lately he has started looming over me, just for fun. He has a sharp wit and poked fun at Hobbit to pass the pedaling hours. We shared a tent for two months on our journey across the U.S., and I greatly enjoyed his company. Amy stayed at home with Charlie's brother, Will, and sister, Annie, for the summer.

Hobbit, aka jon o. holloway: Yes, that's the way he writes his name, in lowercase. (I still don't know why.) Hobbit is an old friend of mine. He picked up the nickname when we were in university together. It's a long story, not worth repeating, but I assure you that he fits the part—not because of his stature, but because of his guile, his sense of adventure, his wit, his love of nature, and most of all, his uncanny ability to connect with almost anyone. Hobbit teaches fine art at Lander University, in South Carolina, takes beautiful photographs, befriends everyone, and travels the world, sharing his joy for adventure along the way. His wife, Lori, kept the animals fed back on their farm in South Carolina while Jon was on the trip.

Annie Holloway: Annie, at 17, is a quiet, thoughtful, and talented observer of the world. I discovered later that she is also quite a strong rider. She is so well organized with her camping equipment and packing procedure that she would usually finish packing and sit in the morning sun reading a book while the rest of us wrestled with our gear. Early in the trip, I tried to match her speed getting prepared in the morning. I couldn't, and finally quit trying.

Erich Bohrmann: Erich has been a dear friend back in our hometown of Yarmouth, Maine, for about as long as our kids have been alive. We met when our children were in daycare together, and we soon discovered that we both like to ride bicycles, ski, hike, and seek adventure. He's a physician assistant at a hospital in Portland, Maine, and requested a leave of absence to go on the trip. When he was denied leave from his job, he resigned. He was that committed. What you will come to understand in the pages that follow is that he is even more adventurous than I originally thought.

Owen Bohrmann: Erich's younger son, Owen, is 15, strong, fit, and quick with a laugh. He also has a big heart and a generous spirit. He lives out loud with his sense of mischief, fun, and adventure. A joy to be around, Owen is often the first to break the moment with a joke and a laugh.

Ian Bohrmann: Ian, whom I often call "What" because it's his most common reaction to anything said to him, is Erich's older son. At 17, he is quiet, noble, and able to ride endless miles with nary a hint of exhaustion. He joined us about a week into the trip because he was back home in Maine playing for the varsity lacrosse team in the state championship. No, they didn't win but had fun trying.

We wouldn't have done this without the kids—we couldn't have imagined it. It would have felt too far, too much of an indulgence, and too isolating to leave the rest of our families at home to embark on this journey.

Annie Hunter, age 11, updated the map throughout the journey

BENDING THE MAP

Although we'd been working toward a departure for weeks, the boys had been dodging the discussion of preparation. Almost every day I would say, "Hey Charlie, you really should ride a bike for at least a couple miles, don't you think? I mean, your ass is going to be killing you."

"Dad, the last thing I want to do before I ride a bike 4,000 miles . . . is ride a bike."

In the weeks leading up to our departure, we had been arguing over the route and debating road choices. It seemed simple when we first came up with the idea: If we started in Seattle, we should point east and start riding, but it wasn't quite that simple. One road choice meant we would not be able to experience a different, separate adventure. It was a paradox of choice. If we chose one route—say north from Seattle into North Cascades Park and over Snoqualmie Pass—we would have been aimed toward Kootenai Forest and magnificent Glacier National Park in northern Montana.

However, that route would be colder and much hillier than other options, perhaps too challenging for so early in the trip. On the other hand, if we started southeast of Seattle, we would cross the Cascades near majestic Mount Rainier and then descend into Yakima Valley. One route choice obviates another, but such is life.

The discussion escalated over email, then spilled into conference calls, then finally a couple of video conferences in which we presented Google Maps scenarios to each other over shared screens. The discussion got heated. You get the idea.

Meanwhile, we had to pack and ship our equipment out to Seattle, our point of departure. Each day, I tried to check something off the list of equipment to purchase or things to prepare. For a week before leaving, I was convinced that I should bring a cycling trailer instead of panniers. I made mental arguments about convenience and storage capacity. In the end, I opted for panniers, as did everyone else, and I'm glad we did. I later discovered how seductively easy it is to overpack and bring too much. During the trip, we stopped on two occasions, in Wyoming and Minnesota, to ship unnecessary items home.

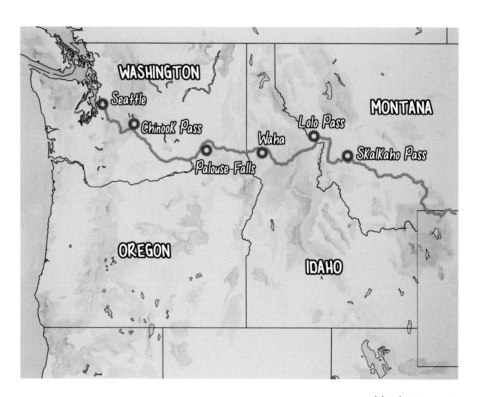

Northwest route

Jorji Knickrehm and Jason Rich

WHEELS UP

We took off from Portland International Jetport, in Maine, with very little baggage. Hobbit and Annie were flying from their home in South Carolina to join us. Most of the gear and bikes were shipped ahead to Seattle, and many boxes, lined up neatly, were waiting for us on the porch of Jason Rich and his wife, Jorji.

Jason has been a dear friend to Hobbit and me since we all attended university together. He and Jorji were thoughtful and gracious to host us for our departure, and I think the volume of boxes arriving at their doorstep surprised them. Jason texted us photos of all the boxes, which contained gear and bikes for six people cycling across country. Once we arrived, we pulled open the boxes and showered his lawn with gear.

This trip has been something of a Rorschach test for friends and family. They say all kinds of things to us: *Wow you must be really excited! . . . I could never do that. . . . What are you going to eat? That's going to take, like what, a couple weeks?* The list of reactions goes on and on.

I think Charlie was getting a little tired of people telling him it's going to be life changing. I asked Ian the other day if he was excited about the trip. "I think it's going to get old," he replied.

Ian may have a point. The trip will likely be many things: exciting, tiring, interesting, frustrating, bonding, challenging, eye-opening, and possibly life-changing. Like life, it will probably be all these things, maybe just a little more compressed.

Willie Weir

ARE YOU ON A TRIP OR AN ADVENTURE?

"Are you on a trip, or on an adventure? It's fine to be on a trip. I love trips. Trips are great. But it's not an adventure."

That's what Willie Weir[1] said last night, among many other things. He lives down the street from Jason and Jorji. Willie and his wife stopped by to join our bon voyage party.

Willie has been cycling around the world for about 35 years. He reckons he has logged about 80,000 miles all over the planet. But he stopped planning "trips" sometime during the mid-'90s.

The last long trip (not adventure) he made was across Canada. He averaged 92 miles a day. He measured and catalogued every elevation gain. He carefully wrote down each road he traversed, every intersection he crossed, and every mile he covered.

But he couldn't tell you much about Canada. He came home to write a story about the trip, but he didn't have much to say other than the mileage he logged and the view from his campsite. Thereafter, he stopped planning trips and started taking adventures.

As he explains it, a trip is when you plan where you want to go, where you will stay, what you will see, the people you plan to meet. That's a trip, but it's not an adventure. A trip is designed intentionally, planned—but an adventure unfolds, revealing itself as you allow the moments and events to change as they occur. You can plan a trip, but an adventure plans you. Willie invited us to think about whether we wanted to take a trip or an adventure.

Sometime yesterday, in the spirit of adventure and on a whim, Hobbit texted an old friend, Mark, who lives in Seattle and asked him if we could all meet at a local brewery, Georgetown Brewing Company. "Meet you there in 10 minutes," Mark writes back.

GEORGETOWN BREWING COMPANY:

This microbrewery, on the south side of Seattle, is listed by Yelp as among the top 10 in a city famous for its 174 breweries (as of May 2017)—more than any other U.S. city.

The relatively young Cascade Mountains extend from British Columbia, in Canada, south through Washington and Oregon to Northern California. The range divides Washington in terms of climate, too, from the temperate rainforest of the wet west side to the dry ponderosa pine ecosystem on the east side.

Minutes later, we're standing with Mark and his wife listening to him explain that he owns a cabin in Greenwater, Washington, on the White River, about 70 miles from here. It's on the Chinook Scenic Byway,[2] in the majestic Cascade Mountains, north of Mt. Rainier.

It's not on our planned route, and we discuss the change over a beer. Our original route was farther south, and allowed for a flatter, easier first day. On the other hand, his cabin—while more difficult to get to because it's higher in the mountains—would be a welcome shelter.

Mark tells us the climb will be a little tough as we approach his cabin towards the end of the ride, but it's worth it. Do we have plans? Would we like to stay there? What would we like for dinner when we arrive?

And this is how the adventure begins: with a bit of luck, and a willingness for spontaneity. Remember all that careful deliberation and route planning? We threw it out the window to allow the adventure to unfold as it chose. With that first chance encounter, we changed plans. We were off to Mark's cabin in the morning.

So it begins.

COLLECT MEMORIES, NOT MILES

Here is another piece of advice from Willie: collect memories, not miles. Finally on the road, we found the first day was long and slow, with a variety of small mechanical issues. A flat tire needed to be repaired, but the new inner tube wasn't properly set inside the tire, so that tube also blew. It's known as a pinch flat—it happens when the person installing the tire doesn't properly set the tube inside the rim; upon inflation, it pinches against the rim and blows out. We won't say who changed the flat, but we were down two tubes in five minutes.

The interesting technical story of the first day of riding was that Owen was slowly grinding his bike into dust over the course of the day. Turns out he had multiple system failures that were gradually conspiring until finally, in the last few miles, he started to complain that his small chainring was loose. It wasn't loose; he had ripped it off with the sheer force of his riding. It was dangling from his bottom bracket.

Owen has a riding style that might be described as attacking, with intermittent bouts of force, then rest. We're in the Cascades Mountains, more specifically North Cascades National Park. During the long climbs up to our camp below Chinook Pass, Owen had managed to shear the bolts off on his smaller chainring. I've never heard of such a thing.

In the process of wrestling with his bike hour after hour, Owen had also managed to wrench his front fork, dislodge his front wheel skewer, and twist his front wheel sideways in such a manner that, for the last 10 miles, it was rubbing against his brake pads. Owen never noticed the problem until he heard the gentle clanking of the loose part bouncing against his bike.

So there we were, at Mark's beautiful cabin on the Chinook River, just south of the entrance to Mount Rainier National Park. Earlier that morning, Erich managed to

NORTH CASCADES NATIONAL PARK: The park spans the Cascade Crest from the Canadian border to just north of Mount Rainier National Park. Highly biodiverse, it hosts nearly 3,000 species, according to the National Park Service: 1,600 plants, 75 mammals, 21 reptiles and amphibians, 200 birds, 28 fish, more than 500 land insects, and 250 aquatic invertebrates.

McGyver a fix for Owen's chainring that featured parts from an old, discarded bike, using a Leatherman, a wrench, and a sewing needle. We're back in motion.

The next day we planned to attack Chinook Pass, reportedly a nasty climb 28 miles straight up from here. It snowed on the pass last night.

ONCE UPON A TIME

June 12

When you hear "Once upon a time," a phrase that is universal in the world, you know what will follow. You don't yet know the people, the details, or the places, but you know a story is about to unfold. In Russia, children's stories open with, in their language, "In some kingdom . . . " In China, "A very, very long time ago . . . " In Poland, "a long time ago beyond seven mountains and seven seas . . . "

Instead of climbing the pass, we decided to stay and enjoy Mark's lovely retreat on the White River. And now this day, stretched like taffy, has opened up and elongated just as those days we remember from when we were 10 years old. We walked through the woods, taking photos of the Ponderosa pines towering over us and finding a tire swing. Erich spent hours tinkering with his bike, his tools, his tent. I wrote a little. Annie read her book by the White River, which ran by the cabin. We all took naps.

When I awoke, I walked the half mile down the river to see what the boys were doing. Rounding a bend, I saw them both knee deep in the sun-speckled water. They had probably spent hours wading in the river, fishing, and turning over rocks as billowy clouds drifted through the sky. I turned my head up and saw individual specks of fluffy, white dandelion seeds drifting and swirling in the wind. I looked again, saw the boys lost in the moment of the river, and thought if I called to them, the interruption would be jarring, so instead I went back to the cabin.

We all biked to the nearby store and bought stuff for dinner. I can't remember exactly when. We played cribbage, made tacos, and sat by the campfire trading stories. There was so much time, and nothing was hurried.

PONDEROSA PINE:

Native to parts of the West and Midwest, the ponderosa pine (*Pinus ponderosa*) can grow to 90 feet and live to 250 years old, according to the U.S. Department of Agriculture. It grows at elevations up to almost 10,000 feet and tolerates drought well. The seeds are the preferred food of 13 bird species, along with chipmunks and squirrels. Its needles are important food for the blue grouse and spruce grouse, and beaver and porcupines dine on the bark.

At one point, Charlie commented, "Jason's house seems like a lifetime ago." It was actually just the previous morning that we had departed his house and climbed into this adventure. And it did already feel like a lifetime ago.

We knew this would happen—that our sense of time would get a little wonky—but we didn't know when or how it would present itself. This sensation of opening a door, of beginning, may be what we all mean when we say, "once upon a time . . . "

INTO THE CLOUDS

The flag guy just laughed. He started with a wry grin and a cackle, which built into a jolly "harrumph." He looked away saying, "You really want to know?"

We were stopped on the Chinook Scenic Byway, just east of Greenwater, approaching the climb up to Chinook Pass. There were cranes and workers ahead. The road was stopped for traffic while they removed tons of enormous rocks that had slid off the side of the mountain onto the road. Our group of six cyclists had wandered to the front of the line of stopped traffic to see what was going on.

I had only asked him, "How is the climb up to the pass?" The previous evening at Mark's cabin, over dinner, Mark had said, "I won't lie to you. It's a bitch."

As the road tilted up, our group spread out a little. Annie, Charlie, and I stayed together, while Owen thoughtfully wandered back to climb with Hobbit, and Erich disappeared ahead into the looming switchbacks.

The climb was about 30 miles. After the first 20, fog set in, the temperature dropped, and snow appeared—at first in patches, then finally in banks towering more than 15 feet above us at the top of the pass. We stopped to take a few photos, but the cold hurried us along and our batteries were dying.

Once the fog appeared and the visibility dropped, we regrouped, doubled up on our blinky lights, and pulled gloves on. The pass was open to traffic, and periodically cars would emerge silently from the fog.

We arrived unceremoniously at the top of the pass. At first, we weren't even sure we were there. The visibility was about 100 feet, so we couldn't see where we were. We parked by a shelter and made peanut-butter-and-jelly sandwiches.

CHINOOK PASS:

At an elevation of 5,430 feet, the pass, which provides the east entrance to Mount Rainier National Park, is usually closed because of snow from November into May, with the opening occasionally delayed until well into June, according to the Washington State Department of Transportation.

BLINKY LIGHTS:

Blinky lights are flashing lights attached to bikes, alerting cars to cyclists. The first bike lights, which were oil-powered, were manufactured in 1876. The industry moved on to acetylene and then batteries by the turn of the twentieth century. Now most bike lights run on alkaline batteries, often assisted by dynamos (incorporated into the wheel hub, for example).

Then we all got a little punchy. Hobbit was wandering around with his camera, muttering about how Trek (the bike company) had screwed us. He had contacted them repeatedly to try to get them to offer a sponsorship for the trip, with no acknowledgment. He held up the jar of Skippy peanut butter and declared Skippy would be our new sponsor. We agreed to all post photos of us eating PB&J with the tag #fucktrekgoskippy. Charlie almost fell down laughing.

That was the first 30 miles. After that, we did the fastest and easiest 65 miles I think I've ever done on a bike. Not only was it 65 miles downhill to Yakima, but we had a tailwind that gained strength throughout the afternoon.

We rolled into the valley as the heat of the afternoon took over. The tailwind had swelled to a steady 25 mph, and the gusts were coming much harder. We laughed, sped on, and drifted among each other for mile after easy mile. We took photos. We coasted. It went on for hours.

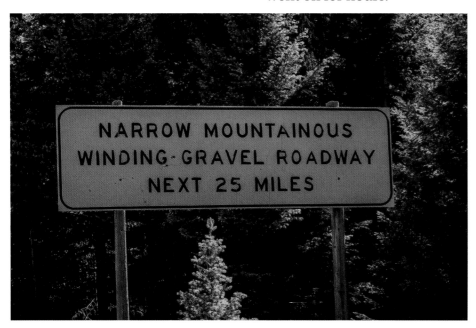

When we stopped, the tailwind was so strong it threatened to topple over our bikes. Owen pulled out a windbreaker, tied the sleeves to his handlebars, and built a spinnaker to pull him along. We took off our jackets and let the sun warm our backs.

By the time we arrived in Yakima, it was late, we were tired, and we made the most unimaginative camping decision of the entire trip. We checked into a Courtyard Marriott downtown and parked our bikes in the basement.

Erich on Chinook Pass, Mount Rainier National Park

Pasco Kahlotus Road, eastern Washington State

FROM PERSEVERANCE TO ELATION

June 15

We were pressing hard to reach Carl's house. No one knew who Carl was except Hobbit, who looked him up on a website: warmshowers.org. It's a site where people register to host travelers, mostly cyclists. Hobbit contacted Carl, who invited us to come by and camp on his farm.

Located at the confluence of the Columbia, Snake, and Yakima rivers, Richland, along with the towns of Kennick and Pasco, make up what is known as the Tri-Cities area in the desert region of Southeastern Washington. The Hanford Nuclear Reservation in Richland was listed by the U.S. Environmental Protection Agency as a Superfund site in the mid-1990s and shut down for remediation.

Today, Tri-Cities boasts of being among "the most popular spots for Washington vacations," according to the Visit Tri-Cities website. Its dry climate, which offers an average 300 days of sun annually, is conducive to a wide variety of sports. In the "heart of Washington Wine Country," the area has more than 200 wineries within a 50-mile radius that produce "some of the finest wines in the world, thanks to the climate and geography of the area."

"Today is kind of an opposite day," Owen said.

"What does that mean?" I asked.

"Well, yesterday was so awesome, ya know?"

Then today, Erich crashed. He was behind us, so no one saw it happen, but the sound was unmistakable. We turned and found him lying on the side of the road, his bike twisted, road rash coloring his arms and legs, a ding on his helmet, and a flat tire. He also fractured one of the small bones in his left hand. He knew it instantly. To this day it still aches when the weather changes.

Erich believed these tiny eastern Washington thorns were the culprit. They seemed to be everywhere. Earlier that same day those little barbs were responsible for not one but two flats. The thorns embed deeply in the tire, and if not carefully removed, they will hide like a stalker and quietly pierce the new tube you insert.

Owen claimed Erich's crash was the low point of the day, but also the high point because we had to stop for a while, and we got to meet a miniature horse and a goat on a neighboring farm.

Annie said the high point was the red, orange, and yellow hues of the early sunset as we rolled up to Carl's house, and the low point was forgetting to unclip her cycling shoes out of her pedals and subsequently tipping over in a parking lot.

Carl works for the U.S. Department of Energy. He, his wife, and a few of their friends live on a five-acre ranch in Richland, with horses, barns, and assorted trucks, cars, campers, and a bus—all in various stages of repair or neglect.

Carl and his wife treated us to a fabulous meal served in their yard under the trees while the sun set. They were gracious, kind, giving, and interested in our travels. And it was a joy to sleep in their field by the barn as the twilight slowly turned into night.

Well, joyful for most of us. In the morning, Hobbit starting barking about his damn "Thermarock," a play on words for his inflatable mattress formally brand-named "Thermarest." Apparently, his mattress had a slow leak in it (perhaps the thistles again?) and had slowly flattened over the course of the night, so in the morning he was lying flat on the ground, thus his insult to the mattress.

A SENSE OF ABUNDANCE

The road has elevated our sense of abundance. Traveling in a small group in these remote, arid plains and valleys has accentuated our generosity and caring. We don't hoard. We share stories. We share snacks.

We got a little piece of advice from Jason before we left his house: "Instead of wondering what to cook with your limited groceries, make the best meal you can each day." True, you will use your best food first, but at the end, when you're out of smoked salmon and fresh bagels, you will always be making the best meal with what you have available.

These past couple of days have created some solidarity within our group. Long silences never become awkward. No one feels the need to interrupt the silence with the sound of their own voice.

Pasco to Palouse Falls was nothing like what we had anticipated. Although I had mapped it carefully on Google, I hadn't examined the topography or the scenery we would encounter. It turns out the road rises to a plateau, where endless fields of grains and fruits are grown.

The road went on and on, undulating through the field, with only the rarest of cars going by. When we finally stopped to rest, we would often just lie in the middle of the empty road, absorbing the warmth of the asphalt.

The hours of open road often stretched out our group, each moving at their own pace, rolling like small little specks within this immense and expansive land. Signs on the fences on either side of the road warned us not to trespass into the rows of corn, wheat, and strawberries.

YAKIMA COUNTY AGRICULTURE:

"Yakima County is the leading County in Washington State in the production of apples, sweet cherries, [and] pears (including Bartlett pears)," according to the Washington State University Extension. Hundreds of acres are planted in peaches, nectarines, plums/prunes, apricots, and other soft fruits. And Seattle breweries don't have to go far to get great hops: "Each year, about 75 percent of the nation's hop crop comes from the Yakima Valley. Although the public may not know it, Yakima is recognized by beer brewers around the world as America's hop mecca," according to *Seattle Magazine*.

PALOUSE FALLS:

The 198-foot falls lie on the Palouse River, about four miles upstream from the river's confluence with the Snake River. On sunny days, the curtain of water often sports a huge, vibrant rainbow. The spot has attracted visitors since Native Americans settled in the area. Geologic forces millions of years apart created the canyon's spectacular, layered basalt cliffs and the dramatic waterfall, according to *Northwest Travel & Life* magazine. Millions of years ago, two massive volcanic flows created the layered basalt columns and varied terraced layers that line the canyon walls. At the end of the Ice Age, about 16,000 years ago, the rushing waters and giant debris of the Missoula Floods, flowing at 10 times the rate of the average river, scoured out coulees, or drainage zones, exposing basalt columns and other geologic formations. Palouse Canyon is one of these resulting coulees.[3] The basalt is layered as much as 100 feet thick, with 200 feet of it exposed at the falls.

We discovered that nothing is open in Starbuck, Washington. There are remnants of a bakery, a bar and restaurant, a post office, and shops, but they are all closed and abandoned now. Everything shut down during the last few years, so we took naps on the lawn in the center of town and ate the rest of our granola bars before working our way nearly 30 miles to Pomeroy, the next town.

STARBUCK:

Founded in 1894, well before Starbucks Coffee, the town of Starbuck can, like the coffee company, trace its name back to the Starbuck family of Nantucket. Today, the town is a quiet, agricultural community with around 120 residents. Most of the businesses have closed, but a hangout for fishermen, Darver Tackle Shop—"the best little tackle shop by a dam site" (yes, there is a dam nearby, on the Snake River)—was still open as of June 2018. The town's unofficial motto is "45 miles from anything you could want to do except see the ocean."[4]

THIS IS WHY WE CAME

June 18

It took 10 gallons of water, 6 beers, some salmon jerky, and huckleberry milkshakes all around to get through the wilderness of the Craig Mountain Wildlife Management Area (WMA), along the Snake River, south of Lewiston, Idaho.

Idaho is nothing but uphill. Ok, we haven't confirmed this on the map, but it sure seems to be.

As impossible as it sounds, and as painful as it feels, we have been climbing since we crossed the Snake River into Idaho. That was noon yesterday. At noon today, we were still climbing. The road turned to gravel, pitched higher, and we took our helmets off so that we could sweat unencumbered in the clean Idaho air. The road continued to lean upward to the sky, climbing through alpine meadows and gravel switchbacks. The landscape was constantly transforming, the flowers and trees changing with the rising altitude.

At one point yesterday, as we labored hour after hour into the sky, a car slowed next to us and rolled down the window. "You know this climbs on for another fifteen miles, right? Do you know where you're going?"

What she was really saying was, "What the hell are you doing? Pull over. Stop. Take a breath and talk this out amongst yourselves. You'll quickly understand you should turn around, find a nice restaurant and a hotel, and rethink this whole thing."

Like idiots, we said cheerfully, "Oh yes, we know. We're on an adventure." Instead of traveling the direct—and flat—US Highway 12, which is a simple, easy route into Kamiah, we chose a divergent path. This took us south around Lewiston, where we ended up on Waha Rd. (County Road 540) and crossed over a pass we decided to call Waha Pass (although I couldn't find a name on any maps) in the Craig Mountain WMA. The route featured desolate roads, ancient abandoned shelters, occasional ATVs, and one very

IDAHO'S WILDERNESS:

According to the Wilderness Connect website (wilderness.net), Idaho ranks third among states in the amount of wilderness acreage. As of October 15, 2017, four percent of the state (4,795,820 acres) was wilderness. Only Alaska, at 52 percent, and California, at 14 percent, have larger percentages and, because of their size, many more acres.[5]

Craig Mountain WMA: South of Lewiston, Idaho, this WMA encompasses 78,000 rugged acres with flora and fauna "as diverse as its habitat and terrain," according to the Idaho Department of Fish and Game. Rocky Mountain Bighorn Sheep had been extirpated from Idaho, but 17 were reintroduced into this WMA in 1983. The species has since "flourished into a healthy population." The WMA is also home to white-tailed deer, black bears, mountain lions, mule deer, elk, many small mammal species, and at least 133 bird species. Local fish include smallmouth bass, crappie, and rainbow trout.

This 180-acre reservoir, at 3,392 feet above sea level and with three miles of shoreline, is administered by the Lewiston Orchards Irrigation District and is part of the Lewiston Orchards Project. It's a draw for fisherman seeking to catch smallmouth bass and rainbow trout and is also known for its ghost. According to the *Northwestern Ghosts and Hauntings* blog,[6] "There is a Nez Perce legend that says there is an Indian Maiden that can be seen walking or sometimes sitting along the shore of this lake."

drunk gentleman who said we were fools to be traveling without a handgun.

This adventurous choice led us to Waha Bar and Grill. We arrived just as they were closing. The welcoming proprietor handed us baskets of peanuts and encouraged us to stand by the fire and throw the shells right on to the floor, where they merged with the piles and piles of other shells that had collected there over time—small mountains of shells, enough shells to trip over if you weren't careful.

After leaving Waha, our adventurous choice led us to meeting Tanner and his wife, Natalia, their son, Cooper, and their two dogs. Tanner saw us on the road, doubled back, warned us of an approaching storm, and then, instead of trying to give directions in these labyrinthine hills,

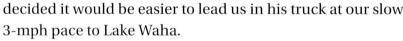

decided it would be easier to lead us in his truck at our slow 3-mph pace to Lake Waha.

Tanner showed us to the lakeside camping spot and left briefly to retrieve a truckload of firewood. He then made a glorious fire and entertained us with stories of local lore while we established camp. Tanner went on about the majesty of the mountains, about how he walked these hills in search of elk horns, about his stints on fracking rigs in the Dakotas, and about life in Idaho in general.

This is the good stuff. This is what we came for. If we had taken the easy route, we never would have met Tanner, or the good bartender who drove down to the lake just to check on us, or the kind soul in the pickup truck at noon who suggested we climb up here.

There's something about a crew on bikes that invites conversation. "By the end of this trip we are going to be a tight-knit unit," Hobbit just said. "Deploy, ride, conquer."

SIDE NOTE:

Here's a common sight—the kids up ahead on the climbs. All of them. I'm a cyclist, and I ride—a lot. I prepared for this trip. Charlie and Owen's training miles for this trip? Zero. None. They went straight from the couch to riding 75-pound bikes over mountains. Annie trained a little, not much, and they are all kicking our ass, leading us through the mountains. Damn teenagers.

LOLO PASS:

At an elevation of 5,233 feet, in the Bitterroot Range of the Northern Rockies, the pass is the highest point of the historic Lolo Trail, which runs from the Bitterroot Valley in Montana to the Weippe Prairie in Idaho. The trail is a National Historic Landmark, designated for its importance to the Lewis and Clark Expedition, and its role in the 1877 Nez Perce War.

THE RHYTHM OF THE ROAD

Dead Man Gulch, Shotgun Creek, Tick Canyon, Dead Mule Flats, Old Man Creek, Fort Fizzle—the names of places we encountered along our trip were awesome, as well as evocative.

We have been climbing for three days—100 miles—up the west side of Lolo Pass from Kamiah, Idaho. It's not an insolent red-line ascent but a steady, unrelenting, constant climb. We're on US Highway 12, which parallels the Clearwater and Lochsa Rivers, so we rise as gently as the river falls.

Our first night climbing Lolo Pass we stayed at Wilderness Gateway Campground, a beautiful spot just 57 miles east of Kamiah. We set up camp and welcomed the arrival of Erich's older son, Ian, who was to finally join us after competing on his high school's varsity lacrosse team in the Maine championship (no, they didn't win, but had fun trying). Ian flew into Missoula, where Erich's nephew picked him up and brought him to our campground to join the group.

Toward the peak, as the road leaves the river and pitches higher, we spread out again. I take up the front position, trying to hold off the kids, who are eager to overtake me on the climb. Thankfully, they were patient and willing to stay together as we pushed for the top of Lolo Pass.

The ride down into Montana was glorious. Annie, Hobbit, and I separated from the group and ran a paceline, drafting each other for 30 miles—all the way down to Lolo—at times ripping upwards of 30 mph, often with Annie leading strong and sure.

We had a moment of calamity at the bottom of the pass. We stopped for a break at a restaurant and convenience store, when a pickup truck pulled in fast and urgent. Two guys emerged from the truck, yelling, "Call 911!" As a medical professional, Erich went

WESTERN PLACE NAMES:

The West is filled with interesting place names, often reflecting the attitudes toward he places of the plain-speaking folks who settled there. Fort Fizzle, in Montana, is an example. A wooden barricade on the Lolo Trail was erected in 1877 by 35 men of the 7th Infantry and 200 citizen volunteers, to stop what Alvin Josephy, Jr. describes in *American Heritage Magazine* as the "great, 1,300-mile fighting retreat" of Chief Joseph during the Nez Perce War. The chief was leading 250 warriors and 500 women and children, along with more than 2,000 horses and other livestock. According to the Montana Office of Tourism, the captain of the fort had clear orders to keep the Nez Perce from passing, but the barricade failed when the Nez Perce, with their horses and possessions, simply climbed a steep ravine behind the ridge to the north and easily walked around the fort. "This maneuver earned White Bird the nickname of the 'Indian Hannibal' and the previously unnamed barricade became a ridiculed 'Fort Fizzle.'"

into full alert and followed them into the store, one man clutching a bloodied shirt tied around his wrist and forearm.

Erich sat the man down at a table in the restaurant and went through a medical inquiry, asking a litany of questions—his name, allergies, and a full incident report—while Hobbit and I assembled various first-aid material Erich requested: gauze, tape, scissors, antiseptic, etc.

Turns out the man was hiking with a chainsaw slung over his shoulder. He slipped, the chainsaw dislodged, and the blade sliced down his forearm, fully lacerating his wrist end to end, cutting a tendon, and nicking an artery, which explained the generous amount of blood. He thought it was the end of him. He wondered aloud whether he would die and asked the bartender for a beer. The bartender arrived with a glass of water, which the injured man rejected, disgusted. Erich assured his patient that he wasn't near death, so he offered Erich a beer also.

Moments later, ambulances, fire trucks, EMTs, police, and even the local sheriff arrived. After Erich had calmly dressed the wound and briefed the medical personnel, we were off like Clark Kent.

That evening, we camped in Missoula at the house of Erich's nephew, Ben. While studying linguistic anthropology at the University of Montana, he rents the house with his girlfriend and generously hosted us.

By this time in the trip, we are beginning to realize that something is happening to all of us. The kids are entering a time of freedom, adventure, and adulthood. And it seems as if we, the grown-ups, are revisiting a lost time—sharing a magical, overlapping moment. It seems as if we are watching our children transform into young adults, while we parents are simultaneously revisiting a younger, more adventurous version of ourselves.

A kindness, a thoughtfulness, has awakened in Charlie. I'm not saying he was a jerk previously, but maybe he was more subdued and didn't openly express the way he felt. Now, in the sanctity of the journey, he's more talkative, relaxed, and thoughtful.

For example, it's become common for him to set up the tent or the camping gear and break it down in the morning, or help prepare meals, or wash dishes. With our limited

UNIVERSITY OF MONTANA:

The flagship of the Montana university system, UM is known for its Nobel Prize winners and ranks seventh in the nation and fifth among public universities in producing Rhodes Scholars, with 28. Its Maureen and Mike Mansfield Library houses the earliest authorized edition of the Lewis and Clark journals. Rolling Stone labeled the university the "most scenic campus in America," and *Outside* magazine called it "among the top 10 colleges nationally for combining academic quality and outdoor recreation."

resources, everything becomes precious, every moment spent intentionally, mindfully. With all the camping chores to do, simply taking the time to retreat from the group and write this feels like an indulgence.

Annie has become braver, more open, more herself. She jokes more, laughs more, goofs more, and rides stronger and faster than ever.

Owen seems to be tacitly acknowledging that his style of riding has been not only destructive to his bike but also an imposition on the rhythm of the group. With his twisting, abrasive, attacking rhythm, he broke his bike again, tearing the rear hub apart and grinding the bearings into bits. We had to replace the hub at a local bike shop here in Missoula. But Owen took accountability for it and stayed at the shop while the rest of us went back to Ben's house for showers.

Later that night, I awoke in the middle of the night to the drunken, and likely stoned, semi-coherent blathering of local college kids admiring our bicycles. In the morning we learned we had all been awake during the event, listening quietly and feigning sleep while we wondered if our bikes and equipment were in jeopardy of being stolen. While awake in the middle of the night, I had a fantasy of leaping out of our tent and yelling maniacally at them, for the pure fun of watching them flee into the night.

As a nonprofit organization, ACA states that its mission is "to inspire and empower people to travel by bicycle." Established in 1973 as Bikecentennial, it is "the premier bicycle-travel organization in North America with more than 40 years of experience and 53,000 members."[7] ACA offers routes and maps as well as guided tours; it also has an online store and publishes *Adventure Cyclist* magazine.

In the morning, we stopped by the headquarters of the Adventure Cycling Association, known as "America's bicycle travel experts," and met the executive director, Jim Sayer, and the delightful staff.

Weighing bikes at Adventure Cycling, Missoula, Montana

Climbing Lolo Pass

MUTINY June 23

The rebellion officially started early yesterday, but it had been simmering from the day before, at Ben's house. Erich's boys were having a blast playing Ben's vinyl turntable, using his Wi-Fi, playing frisbee, and eating pizza. The boys didn't want to leave, and they made that known.

But it was time to go.

We had been riding a bit hard the past few days trying to get to Paradise Valley, south of Bozeman and west of Livingston. The Yellowstone River runs through the valley from its headwaters in Yellowstone National Park. As a reward to ourselves, we booked a big cabin at a place called the B Bar Ranch, in Tom Miner Basin, which branches off of Paradise Valley, and everyone had been working toward that prize. We were going to take a day off, eat, relax, and drink in the beauty of "big sky" Montana.

But the route we picked to Bozeman put half the tribe in a bad mood. We chose a southern route into a valley between the Bitterroot and the Sapphire Mountains—and into headwinds—instead of the flatter, more direct route east to Helena. I wasn't happy about it either, but I kept quiet. I reminded myself to agree; reminded myself that the trip is an adventure; reminded myself about the value of the road less traveled.

Midwest route

Skalkaho Highway (Montana Highway 38) runs for 54 miles between the Bitterroot Valley and the Philipsburg Valley, in the Sapphire Mountains of southwest Montana. This mostly unpaved route climbs through these mountains, and is a "remote and seldom visited part of Montana," says Dangerousroads. org. Along the way, it goes over the Skalkaho Pass, at an elevation of 7,258 feet above sea level. "Originally an Indian route, Highway 38 was built in 1924 to link mountainous mining areas with the agricultural settlements in the valleys," the website adds. Bears, elk, mule deer, badgers, and coyotes are among the wildlife that inhabit the area.

Traveling south and over the Sapphire Mountains added miles, and fighting the headwinds. I told myself that I didn't need plans to go as I wanted them to. I told myself to just relax into the adventure. Erich argued that Skalkaho Pass (aka Skalkaho Highway) would be a beautiful ride through the Sapphire Mountains. He insisted that it would be more scenic, remote, and worth the effort. It turns out he was right, and the journey over the pass and on down into Anaconda was beautiful.

The journey took us through Bitterroot National Forest. It turned out to be every bit as beautiful as parts of Yellowstone National Park, as we found out later, but with the bonus that nary a soul was out there. Few cars passed us as the mountain road turned to gravel, and we climbed past waterfalls and gorgeous vistas in relative peace. We played Tom Petty on our portable radio and drifted across lanes, filling the entire road, as we rode into the mountains.

But Ian and Owen were having none of it. They complained about the route, they complained about the bikes, they complained about the food. Everything was Erich's fault. Even after Owen twisted his chain apart halfway up Skalkaho Pass, and Erich expertly pulled the crank off to unbind the knotted chain and repacked the bottom bracket—by himself, on the side of a gravel road, in the middle of nowhere—Owen still insisted it was Erich's fault the bike broke in the first place.

From the beginning of the trip, Owen had called his father names. He called him "Thick Rick," "Underscore Rick," "Deluxe Rick," or often simply, "Rick." Charlie laughed and encouraged the teasing until Hobbit called a halt to the public roasting.

Once Ian arrived to join the group, the battle ensued again as the brothers turned their attention to each other. In the mornings, Ian and Owen bickered over whose responsibility it was to break down the tent. During the day, they lingered and trailed far behind, halfhearted in their efforts to keep up with the group.

BITTERROOT NATIONAL FOREST:

"A beautiful flower, a beautiful river, a valley, a magnificent range—such is the Bitter Root," wrote Olin W. Wheeler, in his book *Wonderland '97: A story of the Northwest*, published by the Northern Pacific Railway in 1897.

"Leave your stress behind!" says the U.S. Forest Service. "You will find this spectacular 1.6 million acre forest in southwest Montana and Idaho to be a priceless national heritage. Half of the forest is dedicated to the largest expanse of continuous pristine wilderness in the lower 48 states. Much of its beauty can be attributed to the heavily glaciated, rugged peaks of the Bitterroot Range. Drainages carved by glaciers form steep canyons that open into the valley floor. Come enjoy the magnificent mountains, the serenity of wilderness, the miracle of spring flowers, majestic big game, and the sounds of birds here in our land of multiple uses."

The rebellion came to a head this morning. Last night, Hobbit suggested we all get a cheap motel and dinner at a restaurant, which sounded great to me. But Erich wasn't participating in unnecessary amenities. Having resigned from his job to join this trip, he was concerned about his financial situation at the moment. For a variety of reasons, including his budget and a simple preference for camping, he wanted to be outside. He didn't say it out loud, but I also thought Erich wanted his kids to have a more austere experience.

Erich announced that he and the boys would camp nearby and meet us in the morning. Meanwhile, Charlie, Annie, Hobbit, and I checked in to a clean, simple roadside motel. We had dinner at the hotel restaurant, talked, laughed, and played cards into the evening under the wide Montana sky.

We packed and departed in the morning, intending to meet Erich, Ian, and Owen at the campsite to proceed. But early in the morning we passed Erich, who was sitting by the side of an empty highway. He said the boys were still in bed. Ian and Owen refused to break camp, refused to budge, and instead lay in their sleeping bags, simmering with frustration and anger at their father, at the cold, at the situation.

Perhaps they were simply exercising their inalienable right to be teenagers and thumb their noses at the world. Or maybe they were just enjoying their warm sleeping bags in the morning chill. Whatever the reason, I felt bad for Erich and wondered what I could do to help. We said we would wait for them, however long it took, in the town of Anaconda, about 20 miles down the road.

A TREATY IS STRUCK

June 25

DONIVAN'S PUB AND CASINO:

Established in 1985, Donivan's was originally a family restaurant. According to the *Missoulian* newspaper, after experiencing a fire and then a car crashing into the front of the building weeks later, the interior was all but destroyed. It was remodeled in 2016 with a "Vintage Industrial/Steam Punk flair." The owners also expanded the business, adding a pub and casino. The menu now features "14 beers on tap (with an emphasis on Montana microbrews), a rotating wine selection, and spirits and cocktails from Montana distilleries."

Ian and Owen did eventually pack up and ride on to Donivan's restaurant in Anaconda, where we were having breakfast. They arrived at 10:30 a.m. a bit sullen, but willing to negotiate.

A treaty was struck at Donivan's, quashing the insurrection with little opposition. The rebel forces succumbed to a bargain of Subway sandwiches, candy bars, and promises of a shower. The night before had splintered our party, but now we set off together as a tight group.

At one point, we stopped for a break. I called my wife and said we had another 50 miles to ride over the Continental Divide. "Isn't it about 3 p.m. there?" Amy said, sounding puzzled. "Isn't that a little late to ride another 50 miles?"

It was. Nevertheless, we rode from Georgetown Lake to Lewis & Clark Caverns Campground, in Lewis & Clark State Park. It was 92 miles over the Continental Divide, including a surprisingly long climb on Montana State Highway 2 through the pass between Goldflint Mountain and Table Mountain. It was a glorious ride down through canyons and farmlands. We were passed by long, snaking freight trains and finally arrived at the campground at 8:30 p.m.

The following morning, Erich woke his boys again at 6:30 a.m. so we could set off together. They broke camp and sat docilely, munching Cinnamon Toast Crunch with powdered milk. Ian mused that Cinnamon Toast Crunch was, hands down, the best cereal in existence. Frosted Flakes? Not even close. Honey Nut Cheerios? Get that weak sauce out of here. We were back on track: snowball fights at the top of Skalkaho Pass, giant breakfasts at small-town diners, and the endless energy of the kids.

At one point yesterday, rolling into the town of Three Forks, we spooked a deer from the brush beside the road. It set off running through the fields parallel to the road, leaping fence lines while we biked alongside, but quickly started to outdistance us. The boys immediately set off in pursuit, racing ahead to keep pace.

Within seconds, the boys bolted a hundred yards ahead of the group, joyously alive, on a bike, chasing a deer, somewhere in the middle of Montana.

Rolling into Lewis & Clark Caverns State Park, Montana

Paradise Valley, Montana

LIFE IS A DARING ADVENTURE OR NOTHING

We've broken chains, twisted derailleurs, flattened tires, run out of food, got rained out, slept in parks, chased deer, briefly bathed in 40-degree water, climbed numerous passes, and now, another first as we meet a bear.

Five hundred yards ahead, a grizzly wandered around the roadway. We stopped, watching the bear carefully. Behind us, lightning shattered the sky. A thunderstorm loomed, and sheets of rain marched toward us. Then, at that moment, Ian broke his chain, halting our progress. But I'm getting ahead of myself.

Yesterday we left the lovely B Bar Ranch in Paradise Valley and headed south to Yellowstone. The staff at B Bar claimed they have the highest concentration of grizzly bears in Montana. I didn't confirm their claim, but together we started cycling warily down the dirt road that cut through the valley, singing loudly to ward off any bears in the area.

The delightful day off at the B Bar was far too short.

B BAR RANCH:

The ranch "preserves and protects the land, natural resources, property values and associated rights within a unique and extraordinary landscape in the Tom Miner Basin," as its website says. The owners "envision the ranch as an example of a healthy, thriving ecosystem including the human endeavors within it . . . a place of spectacular beauty, committed to protecting its unique and extraordinary environment in perpetuity."

"Established in 1906, the B Bar today manages a herd of Ancient White Park cattle and operates a high-altitude organic garden and greenhouse." The ranch's products feature heirloom varieties of vegetables and herbs and organic grass-finished beef. As the owners sum up the enterprise, "The long days we put in are rewarded with a deeply satisfying way of life and the opportunity to practice the stewardship we preach in a place called 'paradise.'"[9]

We climbed the ridge, took photos of the valley, fished in the local ponds, and allowed the afternoon to drift by.

Thank you, Trina, for the hospitality and marvelous food. Thank you, Mark and family, for shuttling us up the nine-mile gravel climb to B Bar ranch. Thank you, Nicole and Linda, for your joyful conversation and smiles. And good luck to the friendly ranch hand who is off on an audacious adventure to drive to Patagonia!

We went through the North Entrance of Yellowstone National Park, at Gardiner, and headed toward Mammoth Hot Springs among a parade of tourists happily shielded in air conditioning behind the windows of RVs, pickup trucks, and vans. Our destination wasn't far from the north entrance, maybe five miles. Cars passed us graciously as we toiled up the road.

There were hotels, cafes, and trinket stores everywhere. It felt as if we survived a tourist stampede in Mammoth Hot Springs. A park ranger wandered over to chat about our bikes. He told us most of the four million annual visitors to Yellowstone barely leave their cars. It became sport for the boys to pull over at turnouts and point randomly into the wilderness. Within moments, cars would pull over with us and wonder what we were looking at.

We left Mammoth Hot Springs, heading toward Tower Falls Campground, and suddenly found ourselves far from the madding crowd. The sky became dark and ominous, the air turned chilly, and we stopped off to pull out rain gear. On one horizon, a double rainbow appeared, while on the opposite horizon, thunderstorms weighed in on us.

We spun up the road until the cars backed up to a crawl. An adolescent grizzly had wandered near the roadway, then crossed, then crossed again, blocking our path. While the cars rolled down windows and took photos, we slowed and wondered how to pass a grizzly bear on bicycles. Every other car coming towards us rolled down their window and yelled, "There's a bear up ahead in the road!" Yes, we know. The lightning started, and then Ian broke his chain . . . again.

We pulled over. I fixed the chain, and we pushed on, cautiously passing the bear. Then bison appeared. We knew the park had bison, and we were excited to see them, but their size up close was astonishing. At one point in the Lamar Valley, aka the "Serengeti of North America," a bison raked the ground and leered at us just yards from the road. Our

YELLOWSTONE NATIONAL PARK:

Yellowstone was established as the United States' first national park on March 1, 1872. More than 80 percent of the park's visitors arrive during the summer months, and many of them come for the geology and wildlife as well as the hiking and views. The park sits on top of an active volcano and has one of the world's largest calderas (large craters caused by volcanic eruption and collapse).

The park abounds with wildlife, including charismatic megafauna: 67 species of mammals, including bighorn sheep, bison, elk, moose, mountain goats, mule deer, pronghorns, and white-tailed deer, black bears, grizzly bears, and the threatened Canada lynx. Also inhabiting the park are 285 bird species, 16 fish species, five amphibian species, and six reptile species.

Yellowstone preserves the largest herd of American Bison in the U.S., an estimated 4,816 bison (as of August 2017). The largest land-dwelling mammal in North America, the males weigh up to 2,000 pounds, and females, 1,100 pounds. One study indicates they are more dangerous than the park's grizzly bears. While bison may seem harmless and slow, they can, like the grizzlies, be "very dangerous and fast," according to the National Park Service.

BEARTOOTH CAFÉ:

Mystery writer Chinle Miller featured the café in book 8, *The Beartooth Café*, of her Bud Shumway Mystery Series.

strategy for passing bison herds was to blend in with the traffic, attempt to disappear within the herd of cars, and hope they didn't detect our vulnerability.

After lunching by the Lamar River, we left the park through its Northeast Entrance and descended into Cooke City, Montana, in a hailstorm. We pulled over again to put on rain gear, in the hopes of blocking the sting of sleet on our arms.

As we approached Cooke City at the foot of Beartooth Pass, we saw a sign that read, "The Beartooth Highway is Open." Charlie said, "It's concerning when they advise you whether a road is open or not." At that point, it was raining. We got rooms at a fabulous motel, which was also cheap. We showered, ate at the "world famous" Beartooth Cafe, and retired. Tomorrow, we would climb.

It felt like we left Jason's house in Seattle a lifetime ago, but it'd been only three short weeks. Each day is its own universe, its own sacred cosmos. Every day takes both an instant and an eternity. Every once in a while, someone will say, "Remember Wilderness Gateway campground?" or "Remember camping in the Bitterroots?" and everyone is like, "Whoa, that feels like last year."

RELAX, WE'RE NOT ROBBING A BANK

We started the morning at Beartooth Café in Cooke City, where we met the aunt of one of Charlie's classmates from our hometown of Yarmouth, Maine. True story. These kinds of wonderful interactions in which we somehow overlap with people with just one degree of separation happen almost daily.

The climb up Beartooth Highway doesn't start abruptly from Cooke City. We had a few miles of gentle, languid hills and valleys, never knowing when the real work was going to start. When the road turned up, it seemed to go on forever. Annie, Charlie, Ian, and I stayed together through the climb, which lasted nearly 20 miles to the Top of the World Resort.[11] "Resort" is a strong word to use for a small convenience store among a handful of cabins.

As soon as we arrived at the "top of the world" (which by the way, isn't actually the top of Beartooth Pass—the true top, at 10,947 feet, is another eight to ten miles of climbing), we were met by fellow travelers who excitedly warned us about the road ahead.

"You're riding over the top?"

"You can't do that."

"There is about four inches of snow and ice on the road!"

"There's already a truck in the ditch and a motorcycle crash up there."

If all of it was true, what then? We couldn't cycle over miles of thick snow and ice. We couldn't fathom biking back down the way we came, and we couldn't imagine camping at the top, hoping that things improved. It was cold, very cold, with sparse trees and coverage. Plus, the weather was not scheduled to improve.

Among the other travelers was a nice gentleman who introduced himself as "Ranger Al," explaining that he had formerly been an Army ranger. He said he had seen tough

BEARTOOTH HIGHWAY:

This highway, a 67-mile stretch of US Highway 212, has "breathtaking views of the Absaroka and Beartooth Mountains, in Wyoming and Montana," according to Dangerousroads.org. It also boasts 10,000 mountain lakes, 20 peaks reaching more than 12,000 feet in elevation, and 12 national-forest campgrounds.[10] The late CBS correspondent Charles Kuralt, who documented his travels around the country in the TV series *On the Road*, called the Beartooth Highway "the most beautiful drive in America."

adventures. He had endured. He had seen some nasty things out there in the world, but he did not see fit to have us ride through the snow and ice that covered miles and miles of roadway at the top of the pass. He offered to drive one of us to the top to see for ourselves. Hobbit volunteered.

Hobbit disappeared in Al's van for an hour or so while we napped, goofed off, ate, and wondered what our dwindling choices were. The afternoon was aging. We needed a decision soon.

Hobbit returned and announced we were riding. The warming afternoon weather had softened the snow, and the weather was clearing. Everyone groaned, but we mounted up and rode on.

The climb was a literal pain in the ass, but the views were sublime, spectacular, and truly arresting. At one point we met two skiers who were hiking up to ski some lines in the soft, deep snow. We got to talking, of course, and one of them was Amy Rider, a former ski patroller at Saddleback Resort in Maine—another serendipitous interaction. She and Erich, a fellow ski patroller himself, chatted on for some time about all the people they knew in common.

The West Summit was glorious, with ten-foot snowbanks along the road. We rode down the saddle, then up to the East Summit, just when the cold and wind started to kick in. We stopped again, put on everything we owned, and prepared to ride down. Annie's temperature gauge read 34 degrees Fahrenheit. Then it started to hail. The hail pounded our hands, faces, and helmets. At one point, I put a pair of wool socks on my hands.

It took a couple of hours to make the descent into Red Lodge. We found a pizza place, congratulated ourselves, ate too much, and the three dads drank beer. Then, as the light was fading, we started to chat with the waiter about where to camp. He suggested the town park. Why not?

In the 9:30 p.m. twilight of southern Montana, we rolled into the town park to set up camp. The kids immediately protested, "But

Top of Beartooth Pass, elevation 10,947'

what if the cops kick us out? What if they wake us up at 3 a.m. and we have to leave? What if we get arrested!?"

Hobbit was getting frustrated with all the bitching. "Relax people, it's not like we're robbing a bank!" he finally yelled. "We're just going to sleep. If the cops wake us up, they wake us up. We'll deal with it."

In the end, we called the police department and spoke with a kind woman who said she really didn't know but was fairly certain it would be OK. She would tell the local police where we were, so we settled in for the night.

At 4:10 a.m., Hobbit screamed. I know, because I looked at my watch. The sprinklers had come on. Hobbit was the only one who hadn't put the rain fly on his tent, sleeping with just the tent screen open to the sky. He was getting blasted with the sprinklers. He leaped out of his tent, soaked, and started racing around trying to stop the sprinklers with concrete cinder blocks. It didn't work, so then he started redirecting the sprinklers, using the concrete blocks as barriers. He was soaked, ranting, laughing maniacally, and dancing around camp while the sprinklers showered us all.

That's when Owen yelled out in his sing-song voice, "This is what we came for! What a great adventure!"

Camping in Red Lodge, Montana

STRENGTH FROM DEEP IN THE GROUP

Alternate U.S. Route 14 (14A) steeply rises for 15 miles from 4,435 feet in the Powell Valley to the Bighorn Plateau, in the Bighorn Mountains, at 9,082 feet. PJAMM Cycling,[12] a website that ranks and documents the world's top bike climbs, calls it among the "most difficult, hardest, challenging, extreme, best, scenic, inspiring, bucket list climbs in Wyoming."

The day did not turn out as any of us expected, as the entire group was able to summon up surprising strength from deep within.

Lolo Pass was hard, Chinook Pass was hard, Beartooth was even harder, but they were all doable. They were all rideable. With patience, persistence, and a good food supply, we simply had to grind it out.

U.S. Route 14A was something else altogether. It nearly broke us. It was originally a wagon track notched into the side of the mountain in about 1880. The state of Wyoming decided to immortalize it by paving it in the 1960s. It still feels like a goat trail.

Before we left Lovell, we ran into some locals who listened to our plan and started shaking their heads: "You don't understand. The signs say 10 percent grade because it's a Wyoming Department of Transportation ordinance that no road pitch in the state exceed 10 percent, but the truth is that pass is mostly 14 percent. Brakes fail all the time. People go over the side regularly."

The kids were calling bullshit on the whole plan. Hobbit is an optimistic guy, but even he was skeptical. Erich yammered on about the importance of cadence, aerobic thresholds, gear ratios, hydration strategies, electrolyte depletion, conscious breathing to attenuate (he likes that word—look it up) the effects of high altitude, and mental tenacity. It's all useful information, but good lord, he could drive you nuts with that stuff.

WYOMING DEPARTMENT OF TRANSPORTATION'S TAKE ON 14A:

"Highway 14A is extremely steep, a 10-percent grade and more, is winding, has several hairpin turns, and many blind corners. This is a challenging road during the summer season and closed during the winter." For tourists, it is "a beautiful drive" with wildlife, wonderful scenery, and more than 200-mile views in some areas.

As an interesting aside, high-performing individuals often talk to themselves. Einstein famously didn't talk at all until about four years of age and then began talking by first quietly muttering sentences to himself. Studies demonstrate that people who talk to themselves about what they are trying to accomplish are often more successful than those who don't.[13]

I later talked to Erich about his habit of talking out loud. He says it's a manifestation of his own concerns and angst about an impending challenge or problem he's working through in his mind. He resolves the puzzle by talking to himself out loud.

It took about 15 miles riding from Lovell just to get to the base of the climb. The day was hot, and after the first couple pitches up the mountain, we were getting short on water. We pulled over, squinted up at the switchbacks, and chatted about the road and the heat.

Both Owen and Annie declared outright they couldn't do it. It was just too steep, too long. At that point I thought a rah-rah pep talk from me would just piss people off. I pedaled up the road and hoped the group would follow.

I climbed up a quarter mile, pressing the pedal strokes over one by one, the only rest coming at the microsecond between pushing one pedal down and pushing down the other one. It was painstakingly slow. I stopped, turned around, and saw no one following. I looked up the road and saw nothing but up. Those passing by said it went up for at least another 10 miles at this grade.

That was it. Metaphorically, I had my hand on the white flag, my finger on the trigger of the SOS flare gun. I looked at my watch, ready to declare time of death on US 14A, the moment we conceded. I felt as if we had to call it. There was just no way we could all endure this, no way we could drag 75-pound bikes up these grades for another couple of hours.

I rolled back down the quarter mile to the group, crushing the brake levers into the handlebars to stop. There, I found Erich and the boys down in a gully laughing and splashing in a mountain stream. Erich had pulled out his water filter and was replenishing everyone's water bottles with cold, clean water.

We all dunked our heads in the cool stream. Owen announced, "We are absolutely riding over this mountain. There is no way a 10-mile

climb is going to make me turn around and ride 150 extra miles around this hunk of rock. I'm telling you, we are doing this." Owen was adamant. It was inspiring.

Hobbit pulled me aside. "Look," he said, "I seriously do not know if I can climb this thing, but if Owen is doing this, I will try." Annie barked at her dad, "Jon, I cannot climb this!" (She sometimes calls her dad Jon, especially when she's annoyed with him.) Hobbit walked over to her and said, "Buddy, I don't know if I can, either, but let's try."

And so, we tried. In the end, Annie led the way, steady and sure, climbing on ahead of everyone for hours. We took the climb in pitches. A pitch was "to the next turn," or "to the end of that bridge"—probably about a half mile at a time. Near the top, with maybe another pitch or so left, we pulled over and all lay on the warm pavement, absorbing the afternoon sun.

A woman in a Suburban full of kids drove by, staring out the window. As she passed, she clearly mouthed the words "Oh my god" at the sight of a half-dozen cyclists sprawled out like cats on the side of the road.

Just as we topped out, Hobbit flagged down a big truck with a camper. A lovely couple hopped out, introduced themselves, and handed us a round of bottled water and a bag of elk jerky they had made themselves. We started to chat about the camping options. "Just turn left here," the guy said. "Half a mile

Climbing Route 14a, Bighorn Plateau, Wyoming

down is Wyoming High Country Lodge. They're serving dinner. They have showers, bunkhouses, and cold beer."

It was true, and we never would have known about it if not for that kind couple.

The lodge was just inside the boundaries of Bighorn National Forest. The folks there greeted us by telling us to take any beer or other drinks we wanted from the cooler, saying, "We use the honor code here—just write down what you had on the clipboard and pay later." The lodge, which gets five stars on Trip Advisor, Yelp, and Google, also offered a fantastic dinner on their deck, with views of the high alpine meadow in which it stood. Moose passed through to drink at the watering hole conveniently created in view of the guests.

That night we shared the tiniest little cabin, packed tightly with six bunks. Erich slept on the porch.

SANCTUARIES ARE EVERYWHERE

We visited Medicine Wheel this morning, a sacred Native American site located on the highest western peak of the Bighorn Plateau.

While I went up to Medicine Wheel at a civilized hour, after coffee and breakfast, Hobbit and Erich awoke before dawn to visit the sacred site. This is Hobbit's recollection of his experience:

> Erich and I broke camp before dawn and slowly pedaled toward Medicine Wheel, listening to the sounds of nature, feeling our tired legs from the climb the day before.
>
> Just before we reached the summit where the wheel is sited, the silence was broken by the beat of a drum. We approached slowly, respectfully, and observed a family gathered in a circle drumming together. We quietly watched as they played on, and their drumming reminded me of the universal connection between time and space. It felt like the heartbeat of the earth.
>
> From the majestic height of the Medicine Wheel, we could see a panoramic 360 degrees, and while I felt as if I was on top of the world, I also felt as

MEDICINE WHEEL/MEDICINE MOUNTAIN
NATIONAL HISTORIC LANDMARK:

Little is understood about the origins
of this 4,080-acre site, formerly known
as Bighorn Medicine Wheel and officially
listed in the historic landmark registry as
"Annashisee Iisaxpuatahcheeaashisee—
Medicine Wheel on Bighorn River." It is
"a major Native American sacred complex
and archaeological property used by
many different tribes from times before
Euro-American contact to the present
day," and is one of the largest of the
hundreds of stone medicine wheels in
North America, according to the U.S.
Forest Service website. Estimates of the
site's age range from a few hundred
years to more than 3,000 years.[14] The
site predates the Crow nation, within
whose homeland it resides. Medicine
wheels are thought to be used by their
builders for a variety of purposes, from
the ritual to the astronomical. The one
in the Bighorns has been appropriated
over time by New Age spiritualists,
Wiccans, and Pagans.

small as a grain of sand within this sacred place. We walked in silence for over an hour, observing how light interacted on the plains far below.

The landscape was constantly changing as the morning sun rose above the horizon, the shadows raced across the landscape below, the wind carried the voices of jays and magpies in the nearby brush. In the distance, a hawk began to rise on warming thermal air rising from the plain below.

When we were departing, the father of the family broke the silence and said, "My brothers, I have tied a prayer for you." We joined him, watching him carefully tie a prayer flag for each of us to the ropes that encircled the wheel. The three of us shared a beautiful conversation about being interconnected. The thread of humanity is common ground at the Medicine Wheel, and we were reminded that people have made this pilgrimage for thousands of years.

His smile and words will forever be a part of my life. Sacred places bind us in space and time, and I am forever thankful for the gift of friendship.

View atop the eastern edge of the Bighorn Plateau, Wyoming

We took a moment of rest on the eastern edge of the Bighorn Plateau, just before we descended 4,000 feet to Dayton. Looking toward the Great Plains of the central United States, this would be the last time we would be at any elevation until we reached the Appalachian Mountains, nearly 2,000 miles—and a month of biking—away.

This would be our last chance to gaze down from any substantial height, so we stole a few moments to take pictures of the panorama before enjoying a ride down that took over an hour, including stops at the scenic overlooks. Charlie strapped his iPhone to the front of his bike and took a time-lapse movie of the descent.

The landscape had changed. Still almost a mile above sea level, we'd moved into the flat, rolling, arid prairies of Wyoming.

The roads were still long and arduous, but the adventure was becoming less physical, more psychological. The terrain was less momentous, subtler; the panoramas less stunning and grandiose, but more serene. Seemingly echoing the landscape, our tribe had become more meditative, more reflective.

Yesterday the temperature hit 101 degrees. We made an attempt to leave early. We were up, packed, and on our bikes at 7:15 a.m. Today we managed to be on our bikes by 6:45 a.m. We're trying to get up earlier, leave earlier, make headway before the heat of the day. Miles may pass between shade trees here. Yet, somehow in this hot, arid, blank land, there is always some sanctuary inviting us.

In Dayton, after a particularly sad, soggy breakfast, we found the town's sublime little corner grocery store, which served brilliantly crafted sandwiches on toasted homemade bread. A few miles further east, we found Ranchester, hunkering on the valley floor in the oppressive afternoon heat.

●●○○○ AT&T LTE	1:16 PM	✈ 🕐 ❊ 40% 🔋

Mud Butte
Sunny

101°

Sunday Today			101	65
Now	2PM	3PM	4PM	5PM
☀	☀	☀	☀	☀
101°	101°	101°	100°	98°

Monday	⛅	93	65
Tuesday	☀	94	61
Wednesday	⛅	88	62

Tomorrow is the Fourth of July, that great American summer celebration of independence. The Fourth, it turns out, has the highest rate of drunk driving of any holiday in the United States, so after a short debate, we concluded that we would be better off enjoying the holiday in Ranchester and staying off the roads.

We chose the Connor Battlefield Historic site to soak in the holiday. The local boys taught us how to make our way into the Tongue River and float its crisp, cool waters, while the Two Track folk band played on through the afternoon.

It got hot, really hot. Must have been near 100 degrees, but the band played on and the beer and barbecue flowed throughout the afternoon. At one point, Hobbit engaged in a conversation with a woman who claimed she was the great-great-granddaughter of Billy the Kid. It was hard to believe her, since Billy the Kid reputedly had no children. Nevertheless, she was beautiful, and sassy in a cool way. Hobbit politely asked if he could take her photograph.

On the way to Sheridan, to the south, we spent 10 miles on an uninteresting frontage road that ran parallel to Interstate 90. Both Hobbit and Erich can't stand boring roads. I can tolerate them if it's the most efficient route, but Hobbit was having none of it and insisted we turn down a side dirt road suspiciously called "Acme Road." "This route has restricted usage or private roads," our iPhones alerted us. Sure enough, within a couple miles we were confronted by a small river, a tiny bridge, and a locked gate that read, "Private property. No trespassing." As I later found out, this was not uncommon in the vast landscape of the West.

Fourth of July festival, Ranchester, Wyoming

Hobbit again insisted it would be more interesting and fun to trespass and explore, but the kids balked, claiming we would get arrested or shot. Both seemed unlikely. It seemed far more likely that we would encounter no one at all.

I was more concerned about getting lost, so after a few minutes of arguing, I agreed to take the kids back to the "boring" road paralleling I-90, while Erich and Hobbit took the road less traveled. We met a couple hours later in Sheridan, where we refueled at a diner, charged our devices, and picked up some reading at a bookstore before raiding a local grocery to prepare for more miles ahead on sparsely populated roads, which would have few, if any, services or support.

In Ucross, population 25, there is a majestic little church of stone, broad beams, and stained glass, surrounded by tall old cottonwood trees that offer much-needed midday shade. We found the door to the little church open, so we went in and promptly took naps on the cool stone floor.

In Clearmont, population 142, we rolled in to the corner store around 6:30 p.m., determined to have a snack and push on. We entered the store, loud and hot from the road, and asked questions about the road conditions up ahead. The storeowner, Tammy, listened thoughtfully, then gently convinced us to stay in the town church.

UCROSS AND CLEARMONT:

Pam Owen, our editor, who had lived in Sheridan in the early '80s, said that students at Sheridan High School did a series of simple block-print posters of some of the smaller towns in Sheridan County, including Ucross and Clearmont. The Ucross poster just showed a road splitting into a "Y," with the caption "AT UCROSS YOU HAVE TO DECIDE." Clearmont had two posters: one showed three receding rows of four solid-white circles against a black backdrop, with the caption "SEE THE BRIGHT LIGHTS OF CLEARMONT." The other, with a tree bare of leaves except for a single, disproportionately large, green leaf, was captioned "REST IN THE SHADE OF THE CLEARMONT PARK."

Trespassing near Sheridan, Wyoming

Within minutes of discussing her offer, the sky blackened, winds blew the front door open, and lightening rifled across the sky.

At the church, the pastor and deacon came by after their afternoon chores and laid out fresh towels to go with the clean shower they invited us to take inside the church. We all slept among the church pews.

When we open ourselves to them, sanctuaries are everywhere.

The next sections of road—from the church at Clearmont, through Arvada (the stated population was 23 in the 2010 census, although we saw not a soul), Mud Butte, Spotted Horse, and onward to Gillette—were some of the remotest, hottest stretches of asphalt we encountered on the entire two-month trip. While you can find Mud Butte on a map, it isn't a town at all. It's an abandoned building, a dilapidated roadside billboard, and a tree. We ate peanut butter and jelly sandwiches and swatted flies under that tree.

The entirety of the "town" of Spotted Horse is a solitary bar owned and operated by the only two citizens of the town, who make delicious burgers and fries. We gratefully ate their burgers and played Prince on the jukebox before pushing through the afternoon heat into the mining and cattle town of Gillette.

We moved on to Devils Tower, in the northeast corner of Wyoming, near the South Dakota border.

SPOTTED HORSE BAR:

One Yelp reviewer described the bar as being "in the middle of nowhere" while giving it five stars, as did three out of the four other reviewers; the fourth gave it four. "You have not been to Wyoming unless you have stopped at the Spotted Horse Bar," another reviewer, named Jerry, writes. "Colleen and Jerome are great hosts, will tell you about Peter Fonda stopping in, and they serve the coldest beer in Spotted Horse. I have been to Tibet, Mongolia, and even the Empire of Central Africa, but nothing compares to the Spotted Horse Bar."

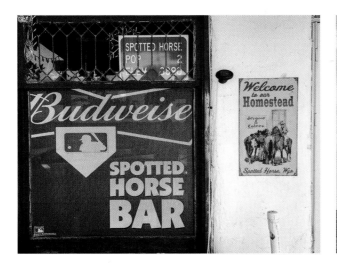

DEVILS TOWER:

The Tower is "an astounding geologic feature that protrudes out of the prairie surrounding the Black Hills" and is considered sacred by Northern Plains Indians and other indigenous people, according to the National Park Service. It's 867 feet high from its base to the summit and 5,112 feet above sea level. Its height and the hundreds of parallel cracks also make it "one of the finest crack climbing areas in North America." Although an Army commander named it on an 1875 scientific expedition, he based his (mis)interpretation of the Lakota Sioux's name for it, with a more direct translation being "Bear Lodge."

GOING LOCAL AT DEVILS TOWER

Somehow, we fit in. Somehow, we fooled them. Maybe it was the weeks of stubble, the sharp tan lines, the salt caked on our shirts. Maybe it was the oddity of three dads traveling with four teenagers, or maybe it was the way we could eat just about anything set near us.

We had wandered into a den of the most hard-scrabble, shredded, world-savvy, kick-ass climbers and adventurers—and pulled it off. We fit in. We were legit.

We just left Frank's place. Formally known as Devils Tower Lodge, it's really Frank's place—Frank being Frank Sanders.[15] He's a legend in the climbing world, and before we met him personally, everyone spoke of him with mythic reverence.

He has been climbing and guiding on Devils Tower for 40 years. He thinks he has climbed it more than two thousand times. Now he has a staff of young climbing guns who take his clients up every day. The food is delicious, the clientele enlightened, the mood spiritual, and the outside shower is only partially enclosed for an al fresco, bohemian experience. Frank plays jazz and blues on the piano before a communal dinner. The price to stay is what you want to offer.

Frank's place is a must-visit stop in the climbing community. His lawn was littered with tents, and filled with men and women of all ages, each tanned and ripped, with calloused hands and strong shoulders. A few were from Australia on a climbing tour, another, from Finland, was interviewing climbers, and one had met Frank while hitchhiking across the United States. The last lad became the cook but was planning his next adventure: to sail across the Pacific Ocean. He said he had never sailed and couldn't swim. Frank's place is full of high-flying dreamers.

FRANK SANDERS:

REI blogger Brendan Leonard met Frank in 2012 to write an article about him and Devils Tower for *Climbing magazine*. "Frank, then 61, drove an ancient car with a license plate reading 'Joy,' chain-smoked Camel filters, slathered everyone he talked to with his buttery charm, and flirted with women from 18 years old to 80, whether or not their significant other was standing next to them," as Leonard described him in the article. "Frank, a climbing guide and bed-and-breakfast proprietor, does not speak; he orates. He talks to you as if you are a room full of people."

CONRAD ANKER:

Anker is "one of the world's most accomplished alpinists," as writer Mark Synnott described him in a 2016 National Geographic article. Synnott went on to write that Anker "is an outlier, a man who has been pushing the cutting edge of alpinism for the past three decades." Four years before, Anker had summited Everest without supplemental oxygen as a member of a National Geographic expedition celebrating the 50th anniversary of the first American ascent. In 2016, then 54, he had a heart attack at 20,000 feet while climbing in the Himalaya. Finally rescued and taken to a hospital, doctors determined he had a major artery blockage. Anker had an angioplasty, then changed to a healthy diet and started meditating to relieve stress. He continued to work with the Mayo Clinic and with Kaiser Permanente on programs to encourage kids to get involved in physical fitness.[16]

Another guy, from Tennessee, was parked out back with his own custom, tricked-out Toyota Land Cruiser and a hand-welded camper trailer he constructed in his spare time. He and his wife, and their uncountable number of kids clambering around the camper, were on their way to hang out at Conrad Anker's house. No big deal. They were just on their way to go chill with one of the greatest climbing legends in the world.

But still, they all nodded solemnly, smiled, and asked lots of questions about where we'd been, where we're going. The kids got lots of questions.

At one point, we had a private conversation with one of the climbing guides, an elder statesman in the climbing community. We got around to asking what the climbing world thought of Alex Honnold's daring "free solo" (without using ropes or other safety gear) climb of El Capitan in early 2017. The guide called it, without question, the most audacious and impressive athletic feat ever. Period.

Today we rode 102 miles, in temperatures topping out near 105 degrees. A local resident told Erich the asphalt temperature can reach 135 degrees, which Erich described as having a blow dryer aimed at your face all day. Tomorrow we cross the Cheyenne River Reservation of the Lakota Sioux, in South Dakota.

On June 3, 2017, renowned rock climber Honnold became the first person to free-solo the iconic, nearly 3,000-foot, granite wall known as El Capitan, in Yosemite National Park. As Mark Synnott writes in a National Geographic article, Honnold's climb "may be the greatest feat of pure rock climbing in the history of the sport... It's hard to overstate the physical and mental difficulties of a free solo ascent of the peak, which is considered by many to be the epicenter of the rock climbing world." Synnott quotes Honnold's take on his amazing, scary feat: "With free-soloing, obviously I know that I'm in danger, but feeling fearful while I'm up there is not helping me in any way," he said. "It's only hindering my performance, so I just set it aside and leave it be."[17]

INDIAN SPIRITS

July 13

The warnings started at Devils Tower. We met Linus, a 20-year-old from Germany, who had saved up for two years for his solo adventure of cycling across the United States. He left New York two months earlier and was on his way to San Francisco. He had a few bike problems, but in short order we (mostly Erich) helped to repair a handful of issues with his bike. It was a rough machine, a wreck from stem to stern. We didn't tell Linus outright, but it was riddled with problems—loose bearings, wheels out of true, worn-out tires, worn chainrings and a stretched chain. Nevertheless, we tightened his hubs, switched his tires, adjusted his brakes, headset, and even tweaked his saddle—to Linus' delight.

Then we started talking about routes. "Oh, you're not intending to ride through the reservation, are you?" he said. "I didn't. I was told it was dangerous. I was told not to go there."

Over the course of the next day, we encountered various locals as we edged closer to the reservation who all said some version of the same thing: "It's full of addicts and thieves. You shouldn't cross, and if you do, don't stay there. Watch your bikes. Be wary."

"Oh, I wouldn't advise you spend the night there, no," the hotel proprietor said. "You'll be OK to cross in the daytime, preferably in the morning, but I wouldn't stay there."

I pressed a little. "Have you been there recently?"

"No, haven't been on the rez for years," she replied. "No reason to."

Hmmm.

We have a habit on this trip of trusting local knowledge. We mine for details about the road ahead—the landscape, the hills, where to stop, where to eat—so we paid attention as numerous people cautioned us about crossing through the Cheyenne River Reservation.

The reservation was created by the United States in 1889 by breaking up the Great Sioux Reservation, following the U.S.'s victory over the Lakota in a series of wars in the 1870s. According to the website of the Cheyenne River Sioux Tribe, the Lakota Nation comprises more than three million acres of "beautiful nature with three major waterways"—the Missouri River, the Cheyenne River, and the Moreau River—and is home to the four bands of Lakota. "Our ancient story begins with living life in peace with one another, living with great respect for our Mother Earth," the website goes on to explain. "Our story is not all about suffering as some would report, but in our hearts, minds and actions our story is spiritual. It tells of freedom, beauty, sharing, healing and hope."[18]

It was going to be 95 miles to cross the entire reservation, from Faith, South Dakota, on the western border, to the Missouri River on the eastern border—95 miles through headwinds. A big day. We woke early, packed extra water, left quietly, and spun the group up to cruising speed.

What we encountered on the reservation was completely different from the picture painted by the locals we had met on the outskirts. On the reservation we received more friendly waves, more horn honks, and more warmth and gentleness in people than we had on our entire trip thus far. It turned into a magical day.

At the first town on the reservation, Dupree, we encountered an older gentleman who leaned back on his pickup truck and told story after story about his history there. He also regaled us about the cyclists he once picked up and gave a lift in a thunderstorm. Further on down the road, we chatted with a thoughtful local Lakota who talked about the Keystone pipeline and his trip to Washington, D.C., to fight the government intrusion on their land.

We came across yet another Lakota, who was riding his horse on the side of the road. He gestured to us and asked if we had water. We pulled over, and Hobbit jumped off his bike to bring him a bottle of water. He drank deeply and reached to hand the water back. Hobbit protested, "No, we have plenty, take more." He took a few more swallows and gave the bottle back. Water out here is scarce and valuable; he refused to take the entire container.

This routine of being approached by waving, friendly honking cars went on for hours—until late afternoon, when we approached the Missouri River. The sun was drifting low in the sky.

Up ahead, an immense Lakota approached us, striding intentionally toward our group on the shoulder of the road. He was tall, strong, with long, jet-black hair. I was unsure what to do, so I drifted toward the middle of the road to ride around him. He adjusted and continued to walk straight at us, holding something in his outstretched hand.

We slowed, then stopped before him. He locked eyes with me, then Hobbit, then the boys, and then Annie. He handed me sprigs of sagebrush. "This is for you, my brothers and my sister. This is for safe passage beyond our land. Be safe, my friends."

And then he turned, walked to his car, and said, "I will guide you across the border." He started his car and rolled slowly over a hill just beyond our sight. When we reached the top of the hill to peer over, he was gone. He vanished, like a ghost, like a whisper.

Chasing dawn, South Dakota

And just like that, we rode together across the Missouri River, blessed by those who had shepherded us through the Lakota homeland.

There is a small motel and campsite on the east side of the river, called Bob's Resort. We had dinner admiring the wide river, slept, and moved on in the morning through Gettysburg, South Dakota—"Where the Battle Wasn't"—and then further on across the plains of South Dakota, propelled by strong tailwinds.

Hobbit and I had downloaded an app to our iPhones that gave us current wind direction and speed. Here in the flatlands of America, wind makes a big difference. When it's in your face or pushing you to the side, the wind can be an exhausting torment, if you allow it. Instead of fighting the wind, I try to pick a comfortable pedal stroke and ignore our glacial speed.

But when the wind is at your back, like today—strong and gusting to 40 miles per hour—Erich and I decided to use it to our advantage, and ride as fast as we can. At times we were riding steadily in the high 20s and covered the 50 miles to Faulkton in just three and a half hours—on a searingly hot afternoon, no less. We stayed in another motel to escape the heat. Word spreads fast in these small towns, and within a few hours a local reporter had arrived to do an interview with us in the hotel lobby. Ian and Owen declined the interview, citing a lack of clothing to wear. They remained in their hotel room, naked, as every last stitch of clothing they owned was in a washing machine at the moment.

The next day, we pushed on to Clark, 80 miles from Faulkton. Now the landscape was changing yet again, with the rolling, unbroken, treeless plains giving way to a leafy horizon of maple, oak, willow, and more.

In lovely Clark, we discovered a town park, where the locals invited us to camp. We cycled a few blocks over to the local public swimming pool. We relaxed in the pool's cool water, watching the local kids perform stunts off the diving board. Charlie, Ian, and Owen

took a few turns sharing tricks of their own. After the pool, we prepared dinner on picnic tables in the park and watched a local youth baseball game unfold under the lights.

The following morning, at Heather's Bistro and More, a fantastic diner, we had yet another interview from a local newspaper reporter. Feeling like celebrities, we were beginning to get our standard patter down for the interview. Hobbit said something about finding the beauty of the people of the heartland, I said something about sharing adversity with our kids, and Erich said a few words about embracing uncertainty. We were starting to inhabit our new identities, and as Kurt Vonnegut put it in the introduction to his novel *Mother Night*, "We are what we pretend to be, so we must be careful about what we pretend to be."

From Clark, we rode on to Clearlake, where we purchased charcoal and attempted to grill a full meal of hamburgers and vegetables. It seemed to work pretty well, up until the

CLARK, SOUTH DAKOTA:

According to the town's website, Clark is "Home of Potato Days, featuring World Famous Mashed Potato Wrestling!" In 2017, the town was planning to celebrate its 26th Annual Potato Day in August. "The potato is king" in Clark, "where local farmers grow bushels of the tasty tuber," the website says. "That's why, each year, the town throws a party in honor of its favorite over-used, under-appreciated starch," which apparently Mr. Potatohead is "proud of." While "the locals vie for top honors in a Best Decorated Potato Contest," and "Potato Dish Cooking Contests always bring out the best cooks in the county," the highlight of the celebration "involves grown adults wrestling each other in mashed potatoes!"

moment Hobbit argued we should put the cooked hamburgers, with buns, in a plastic bag for a few moments. He claimed it would soften them up. Whatever.

The boys have softened their approach to Erich, and have largely left him alone since he stopped harping on the perils of heat stroke and dehydration. Well, that was my interpretation. I later learned from Erich that he hadn't stopped worrying about the heat conditions, just kept his opinions to himself once it seemed the rest of the group was impervious to his sound clinical reasoning. I suspect our ignorance of the dangers of heat exposure was even more maddening to Erich.

Keystone XL Pipeline,
Cheyenne River Reservation,
South Dakota

In the past week, trees have arrived on the landscape, along with cooler air, which has made the days and evenings pleasant. Now the boys have turned their attention to goading Hobbit to tell stories about growing up in the South. Charlie will ride next to Hobbit for hours and listen to tales of his young adventures chasing catfish and hunting in the woods of South Carolina.

Two days down the road, we enjoyed a special evening with friends in Chaska, Minnesota. Amy Weldon, her husband Brian, and their two children treated us to an amazing evening of conversation, endless snacks, gourmet barbecue, craft beer, satellite television, laundry, and air conditioning. I think we ate just about everything in their house, including all of their boxes of cereal.

Their young boys wrote a welcome sign in chalk on the driveway and were delighted to spend time with our older boys. They played, wrestled, and watched *Pirates of the Caribbean* together. We didn't want to leave.

KIDS RAISING PARENTS

The truth is we would not have done this without the kids. We know people do. We've run across young couples, older couples, and solo adventurers on bikes. We just met Uli while camping on the shores of the great Mississippi River. She is cycling from Fairbanks, Alaska, to Florida with her dog riding in a child's trolley behind her bike. Seriously. But we have never met any groups with kids cycling across the country. I can't envision this trip without our children, and neither can Hobbit and Erich.

There was an urgency in doing this with the kids, a timeliness. The window is small. Somewhere between about 16 and 18 years old, they are old enough to physically do just about anything, and young enough to be willing—or maybe just susceptible enough to suggestion. If we had waited, even another year, they would have told us to go jump in a lake. They might have told us, "Hell no, we're not doing this."

We dads embarked on this trip to give the kids an opportunity to learn things about themselves that we couldn't teach them directly. We can set up the circumstances and the environment, but there are things that kids need to learn for themselves. Patience, for example. We can say, "Be patient," but until you *have to* be patient, you don't really learn patience.

Uli and Jackson, cycling from Fairbanks, Alaska, to the Florida Keys

Or tenacity. We can tell our kids to be tenacious, but until they *have to* grind through a 15-mile climb up 6,000 feet, or slog through 10 miles of headwinds, they might not know what tenacious means, or at least what it means to them. It doesn't take a bike trip to encounter these adversities, but it's a useful and interesting way to learn.

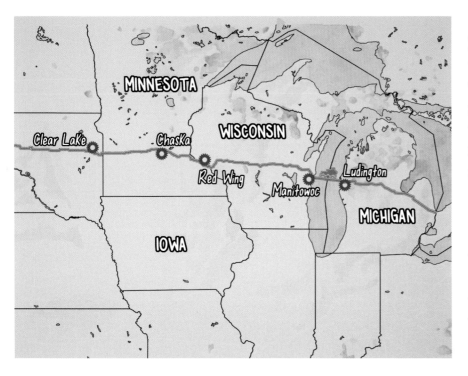

Central route

When we spend six to eight hours a day on a bike together, we get the chance to wander throughout the group and have independent little conversations with different people. These mostly occur in small, private moments in the middle of the day, particularly if the road is quiet. Yesterday Hobbit, Erich, and I started a discussion about what the kids are teaching us.

"What are you learning from your kids?" I asked Erich. He had very clear answers. He learned that being an only parent requires punctuality and rigor. He and his wife divorced when the boys were very young. She was entirely absent from their childhood, and he was determined to be a successful parent, but it took discipline. At home, he would awake a little after 5 a.m., make breakfast and lunches for his kids, drop them off at daycare promptly at 7:15 a.m., then head to work. He had only 45 to 50 minutes in the afternoon for exercise before he picked them up again at 5:15 p.m.

Out of necessity, Erich's life revolved around reliability, punctuality, and being dependable. So now, on this trip, his boys want to screw off, sleep in, linger at every rest stop, and generally resist his instinct to march through every day. And as a result, he's relaxing, he's letting go. Erich is slowly allowing the trip to unfold how it chooses to unfold, even if that means sitting idly by while his boys bicker with each other or drift through portions of the day.

Hobbit had a different kind of answer. He is an easygoing, good-natured person, and typically welcomes adventure and challenge, but he admits he can get irritable. He can gnash his teeth at the traffic, or grumble at the wind. He doesn't care for annoyances. He says Annie is teaching him to relax about them, to not take the little things so seriously.

Annie has a brilliant strategy she uses to make Hobbit think about circumstances differently. "Just pretend it's a movie or a play, and all of these people are actors playing roles," she'll say. "Imagine the backstory of the waitress, or that couple over there. Imagine how their morning went before they arrived here." Hobbit says it helps him find context, think of broader stories, and stop getting frustrated about the small things that don't fall quite the way he wants them to.

Parenting makes you want to be the person your dog thinks you are—a better version of yourself, with more integrity, more stature. But the truth is, what do we parents know? We're just winging it, too.

It seems to us the way to develop a stronger relationship with our kids is not to instruct, but to simply model the path. I'm trying to let go of being right, trying to relinquish the need to have all the answers. I'm trying to let go of telling Charlie how to pack his bags, how to ride intelligently, or what he should be eating to stay healthy on this trip. I'm trying to show him I trust him—that I know he's a smart kid who will make good decisions.

It's not always easy, of course. I still bark at Charlie when it looks like he's doing something stupid or unsafe on a busy road, or treating his bike in a way that might damage it, because breaking a bike means an inconvenience for all of us. But, for the most part, we're trying to give trust. It seems the only way to get him to treat me with respect is to give him the respect he needs to make his own decisions.

This trip has become a series of small moments of letting go, of giving trust, and the accountability that goes with it.

THICK AS THIEVES

We're in eastern Wisconsin. The landscape is changing yet again, now drastically different from where we were just a week ago. Then, we were in the high, arid blast furnace of Wyoming plains and prairies, constantly searching for our next drop of water. During that period, we each carried at least four liters of water and still ran out every few hours. Those were the days of Spotted Horse ("population 2"), Wyoming, and Faith, South Dakota. Those were the days of scanning the horizon for trees.

There is a stretch of road east of Belle Fourche, South Dakota, that is so desolate and unpopulated that we rode straight out for most of the day before encountering water or food. The locals advised us that rattlesnakes like to sun themselves on the road: "Just pick your feet up when you roll past."

Now, in Wisconsin, there are convenience stores, pharmacies, grocery stores, pizza shops, and more every few miles. Yesterday, we stopped at a Target for the sheer delight of wandering for an hour in an air-conditioned ocean of consumer goods. The boys went to the electronics section and played Xbox.

And curiously, we're eating less. A few weeks ago, we would roll in somewhere and devastate plates of nachos, hamburgers, pizzas, sodas, ice cream. We didn't discriminate—we would lay waste to anything edible. The appetite is still there, but we're not quite as ravenous.

Now, the homing beacon is getting stronger. The roads are simply wonderful—long, languid stretches of paved country roads, and we're preparing to board a ferry across Lake Michigan. The kids have been looking forward to this for days. We get to travel about 65 miles across the lake without pedaling at all. The ferry takes a little more than four hours—four glorious hours of moving along at 15 mph without touching a pedal.

"Good roads paved the way for Wisconsin's rise to the top of the dairy world a century ago," according to the Wisconsin Farm Bureau's website.[20] "Milk needed to travel from the farm to a bottling plant or cheese factory and on to the customer in short order. This meant gravel gave way to hard-surfaced roads in rural Wisconsin. Today, milk's prominence remains. Dairy products contribute about half of the $88 billion that agriculture contributes to Wisconsin's economy each year. Dairy's economic importance to Wisconsin is more than what potatoes mean to Idaho, and citrus means to Florida, combined."

We swear like sailors now. Nothing is beyond our reproach. We curse the wind, the road, the cars, the heat, the food, our bikes, even each other. Anyone might be mildly shocked to enter one of our conversations as we ride for hours among the backcountry roads of Wisconsin and Minnesota. We color our expressions and descriptions with all sorts of creative invectives. Hobbit and I have been having rap battles. For the uninitiated, a rap battle is a rhyming competition in which the goal is to creatively insult each other as much as possible, in rap fashion.

When the boys started swearing—probably back on the hot, interminable roads of Yakima Valley in Washington State—it didn't really seem inappropriate. It felt like they were just expressing their own piece of mind in a safe environment. I was reminded of studies that suggest people who swear tend to be more honest than those who don't.

The group can turn it off quickly when we enter social environments and be polite and thoughtful when we interact with the many people who wonder what in the world we're doing. But once we enter the safe confines of rural roads, the language gets increasingly colorful. Recently I've tried to goad Annie into cursing. She almost got there. I think maybe we even got her to say, "Damn!"

This notion of small, tightly connected groups traveling together led me to a University of California study[19] of astronauts navigating the psychological aspects of working

together. According to the research, the social dynamics of small groups in isolated environments is characterized by three stages. In the first stage of the journey, participants find social similarities. In stage two, they find common dislikes and share their mutual displeasure. And in stage three, they find a common, unifying vision.

Our unifying vision is to share this tremendous experience together, and also to anticipate the joy of ending at home with friends and family.

Tom Schrag

PROFANITY STUDY:

A team of researchers from the Netherlands, the U.K., the U.S., and Hong Kong conducted the study, reporting the results in the journal *Social Psychological and Personality Science*. The results indicated that "profanity was associated with less lying and deception at the individual level and with higher integrity at the society level."[21]

IN THE TIME OF STORIES

OMG. Ian just took Owen's shoes and put them directly under the campsite water faucet at full blast. Then Owen took Ian's shoes and scooped mud into them. Then the brothers took turns attacking each other.

What set them off was the news this morning that we cannot cross into Canada at Port Huron. We have been riding for about three days to reach Port Huron to cross the border there. We just called the Port Authority, and they said they do not permit cyclists over the bridge because it's an interstate highway, and we aren't permitted to use the pedestrian bridge either. Instead, we have to ride 30 miles south to cross the St. Clair River on the Bluewater Ferry to enter Canada.[22]

Fast-forward a few hours, and our information has changed . . . yet again. It turns out we *are* permitted to cross the international Blue Water bridge at Port Huron, although "riders and bicycles will be transported at the convenience of the Authority," according to the Michigan Department of Transportation website. After several phone calls, we received vague assurance from the Port Authority that they would take us across the bridge if we arrived at 7 a.m. tomorrow morning.

That means we got to spend the evening in lovely Port Huron, near the Port Authority, dining on Mexican food and watching a movie at the local theatre. In one wonderfully comic moment at the restaurant, Hobbit and I ordered margaritas. Erich commented he had never had a margarita (or tequila, for that matter) in his life. So, we promptly ordered one for him, and after drinking it and declaring it delicious, he started to giggle and claimed his face was going numb.

The kids started to rant because they are pushing hard to get home. In a turn of events, now they are asking to do 100-mile days. A few weeks ago, they wanted to start late and

quit early. Now suddenly, the pull homeward is strong and the kids want to crank out the miles. They don't even get tired. I mean, they do get tired of biking, bored with it—but they don't seem fatigued by it. Punks.

Each day is new. Each day is uncertain. The only certainty is that we will wake, pack, and begin riding again. Whom we meet, the weather we encounter, the people we interact with will all be new. There is no familiarity, except the deepening relationships with each other. Our group is tight, thick as thieves, but everything we encounter each and every day is always new.

It's the same reason we describe previous days as seeming so far away. For example, we can recollect our experiences in Gillette, Wyoming, but when we do, it feels like a distant memory. So much happens in each day. Every day is so rich, dense with experience.

So, if we tell you that nothing happened today (or yesterday), it doesn't mean that *nothing* happened today—it only means that we've normalized our daily rhythm in the same way that we might think of our morning coffee, our commute to work, and our evening dinner if we weren't cycling 80 to 90 miles every single day. It's just what we do now. It's how we live.

Not every day is a seismic, rapturous experience. Earlier today I mentioned to Annie (after only 50 miles) that I was done, tired, and ready to finish for the day. We still had 40 miles to go. "Today I was ready to be done after breakfast," Annie responded.

While we don't feel the bike trip has become mundane, it has just become more routine. Today we turned onto a road to take us six miles to our final campground destination. The road was closed. Signage and construction equipment everywhere. We surveyed the scene and found a small, rickety wooden bridge we could use to walk our bikes around the bridge construction. This is the kind of break that makes the trip more of an adventure, less routine.

The most interesting parts of the day are often the small moments—trying out the massage chair at the mall, juggling a soccer ball by the side of the road, spectating as Ian and Owen do battle with each other at the campground, or just watching Hobbit strapping salad tongs on his handlebars.

Somewhere in the middle of Michigan, Hobbit started on a rant about the stupidity of standard handlebar design. His road bike came with the usual drop-bars installed on most road bicycles. Hobbit thought the design was idiotic. In his opinion, he was left with only two choices—leaning over to grip the top of the bars, or leaning over even further to grip the lower drop-bars. He wanted an option to reach the handlebars while sitting upright, instead of hunched over. He had developed callouses on his hands and an ache in his neck from being forced to use the handlebars provided. His solution was to purchase salad tongs, and a roll of duct tape, and strap them on his handlebars, sticking straight up.

The resulting sight was truly comical—Hobbit sitting upright and tall, smiling and gripping the ends of his salad tongs while riding the sunny bike paths of Michigan. The boys roared in laughter.

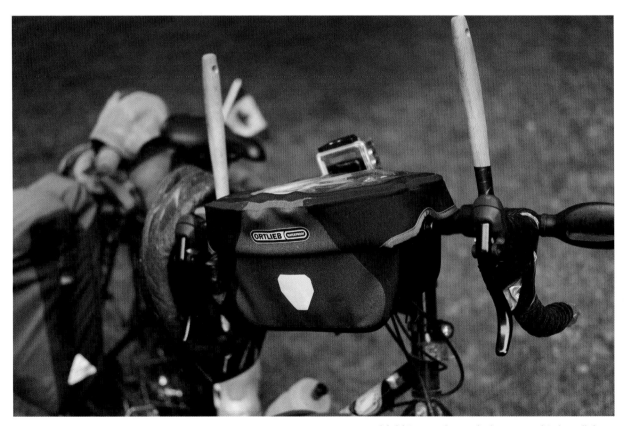

Hobbit attaches salad tongs to his handlebars

IT'S HOW WE RESPOND THAT MATTERS

It's not what happens, it's how we respond. It's not what happens, it's how we respond.
I kept saying this mantra to myself while fixing Charlie's bike on the side of the road. We had a late start, then got sucked in by a lovely bakery where we ate tasty éclairs, and now we were burning yet another hour on the side of the road because Charlie destroyed his bike. I got impatient.

We've been at this for more than 3,000 miles. He should know better than to cross-shift both front and rear derailleurs simultaneously while applying maximum torque as he is standing and cranking up a steep hill. The whole drivetrain blew. The front derailleur twisted, and the chain contorted into a Gordian knot. The whole damn thing was locked up. It took almost an hour to reset the derailleur collar, adjust the cable tension, etc. It was all avoidable. I blew a gasket myself.

What made me crazy was that the whole situation could have been prevented if he simply treated his bike with more respect, rode it a bit more gently. (Here comes the lecture . . .)

I ride a 1992 Bridgestone RB-T bike. I replaced the chain and rear cassette five years ago. I have old-school cantilever brakes. I've replaced the tires, of course, and the rear wheel, but the front wheel is original. I have no problems with my

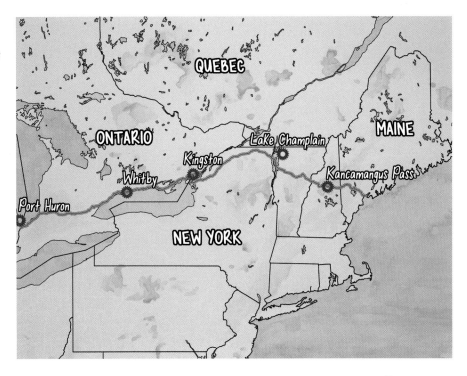

Eastern route

BRIDGESTONE RB-T BIKE:

Bridgestone's RB-T (for "Road Bike–Touring") was introduced in the early '90s. "The RB-T, brainchild of cycle culture legend Grant Peterson (founder of Rivendell bikes), has somewhat of a cult following these days, and is becoming increasingly difficult to find," says the Brazen Bicycles website. It's designed for fast touring, or randonneur, and long-distance endurance touring.

bike. None. I treat it with care. I'm supposed to be learning patience, but Charlie's lack of care with his bike set me off.

Erich, meanwhile, has become the Zen master, or Obi-Wan Kenobi. He doesn't care when we start, how long we break, or where we end for the day. If someone breaks their bike, he simply pulls over and helps to fix it. He's been true to his promise of allowing the adventure to unfold the way it chooses. Obi-Wan also sleeps precisely 18 minutes in the middle of the day, wherever we happen to be.

Like me, talking about my own beautiful traditional touring bike, Erich has also been prattling on about his bike for weeks. It's utterly and completely unlike my bike—well, unlike most bikes. It's a custom-made Jones Bike[23] that looks like a zombie at the prom. If you ask—or even if you don't—he will give you a tour of this aberration, which has a strange truss fork, wrap-around H-handlebars, fat-ass tires, White Industries hubs (who cares?), and apparently, an endless supply of gears. Whenever anyone runs out of gears on these climbs, he will happily announce he still has three or four more to go. After one such announcement, probably up Skalkaho Pass, I commented that if he always has gears to spare, he overbudgeted on gears.

Erich has such an affinity for his bike that the boys have taken to calling it the "Bitchin' Jones." As in, "That road is no problem for the Bitchin' Jones." Or, "Whoa, don't park so close to the Bitchin' Jones."

Erich, as I've noted, is something of a purest about the trip, which means sleeping outside as much as possible and taking the road less traveled. He particularly likes unusual, out-of-the-way roads. We all do, but Erich is more than willing to ride god-knows-where to catch a view or an interesting climb.

So, yesterday, after we had squandered pretty much the entire morning and had ridden only 40 miles by 2 p.m., the kids noticed that, as we approached Toronto, we were riding alongside a train. At one point someone asked, "Where does the train go?" I explained it was a light-rail commuter train and—wait, hang on, let me check—yes, it looks like it goes for another 50 miles east, through the city, paralleling our current route.

Eureka! The kids conspired to get to a train station. So, we walk into a train station, ask a few questions, and discover we can take our bikes onboard. The train also goes right to the house of Jen O'Brien, a friend of mine who generously offered to host us for the evening. *But* her house was more than 70 kilometers away (we're using metric now that we're in Canada, eh?), and it was already after 3 p.m. Plus, honestly, we've all gotten a little weary the past couple days. As Owen reminds us, "Everything is awesome except the biking."

The fact that Erich was not only willing but sincerely enthused to ride a train across Toronto for 70 kilometers was remarkable. The kids were overjoyed.

After a couple of marvelous hours riding a train (I read my book), suddenly we're at Jen's house. She has made a glorious meal; Don, her husband, is providing a steady flow of beer; and the boys in our group are in the basement with PlayStation. We stay up late talking, the kids jump in the pool, and we sleep under the stars on her back deck. Life is good indeed.

Now we're in Ontario. It's lovely—800 kilometers (about 500 miles) to go.

Visiting Jen and Don O'Brien, Whitby, Ontario

LIVING FORWARD

We crossed back into the U.S., again by ferry, from the cool city of Kingston, Ontario, and cruised across upstate New York to Canton. At the delightfully cute Cape Vincent, New York, border crossing, there were just two border officers to greet us as we disembarked the little ferry. They inquired about our travels and asked if we had anything to declare. Erich volunteered that he was in possession of an apple. The border agents asked him to eat it.

The following day, we awoke again before dawn and raced more than 100 miles across the entirety of New York to Plattsburg, just on the west side of beautiful Lake Champlain.

We smell the barn, so to speak. We're close—within striking distance. Tomorrow morning, we get to ride a beautiful rail trestle into Burlington, Vermont. We are roughly 250 miles from home, depending on what route we choose. Once we cross into Vermont, we will begin to know the roads, know the way home. Barring mechanical failure, or succumbing to saddle pain, we will roll into Yarmouth, Maine, in just three days.

Back in Ranchester, Wyoming, we encountered a group we chatted with for a while. "What y'all are doing is impressive," one guy said, "but it's not the bears in Idaho, the bison in Yellowstone, nor the climbs over them mountain passes that scare me. What frightens me most is that little seat y'all spend all day on."

ISLAND LINE BIKE TRAIL:

This 13.4-mile trail runs from South Hero to Burlington, crossing Lake Champlain on the "spectacular" three-mile Colchester Causeway, according to the TrailLink website (traillink.com). The trip requires a ferry ride to cross a 200-foot gap to destinations on South Hero Island. Riding the trail, bikers can enjoy views of New York's Adirondack Mountains across the lake and 14 granite boulders in Burlington's Earth Clock, which create a calendar, clock, and compass—"an example of this town's artistic reputation," as TrailLink puts it. A local nonprofit group, Local Motion,[25] whose mission is "to bring walking and biking within reach for all Vermonters," manages the bike ferry, charging a reasonable fee for trips.

Lately, we have been throwing down weeks where we bike for 500 or 600 miles, like the pace we were doing to get across South Dakota. We ripped across South Dakota in four and a half days. We felt an urgency to move through that land, finding it glorious and beautiful, yet often sparse and desolate. We slowed a little through Minnesota (yay, the tour of the Prince studio! Yay, the stop at the Weldons' house!), and once we got close to Minneapolis, we had to deal with stoplights and traffic, which again made for a more meandering pace.

Avoiding busy roads, we have found many marvelous rails-to-trails bike routes since we left Jason's house back in Seattle. Of the 3,200 miles we have ridden thus far, we have found untold bike trails—each interesting in its own unique way. We found brilliant trails in every state, notably the Pere-Marquette[24] in Michigan. On that day we got lost in conversation and scenery for hours. And just this morning we biked the Island Line Bike Trail, bordering Lake Champlain.

The composition of the group during the day is changing. Obi-Wan will sometimes leave early, sometimes stay with us, but is always on the move. He wakes, and by the time I have a cup of coffee, he has already patched a tire or cleaned a chain. He eats nuts and berries and naps under trees while we dine on club sandwiches at the local diner. Obi-Wan is at one with the road.

Now we are in Burlington at a cafe, waiting for Obi-Wan and Owen to catch up. Owen had a major mechanical malfunction a few miles back. I think a pair of his shorts slid off the back of his bike and jammed into the rear brake, bending the rotor.

The moment his brake suddenly locked up, Owen happened to be at the front of the group, so his slamming on the brakes had the jarring effect of making us all quickly swerve in a panic to avoid crashing into him. I yelled at him until I realized it was entirely accidental.

Obi-Wan and Owen arrived half an hour later, after Obi-Wan fixed yet another mechanical issue. It isn't unusual for the group not to wait in that circumstance and just split up instead. Lately we often drift apart during the day. We joke that sometimes it's like *The Amazing Race*, the TV show in which teams travel from place to place any way they possibly can.

Everywhere we stop, people ask us questions. Ian is usually quiet and doesn't talk a lot, so lately we've been getting him to explain what we're doing. Most people think what we're doing is not necessarily impossible, but impossible for them, beyond their reach. People everywhere tell us they could never do it.

Hobbit and I have been reflecting on two ideas. The first is, we demonstrate that it *is* possible. It just takes one mile at a time to get it done. And the second is, we aren't all as indispensable as we might think. Life goes on back home. My own business still operates, with me checking in periodically from the road. Hobbit's studio business still runs, and events are still hosted back home at his work. Patients still get good care at the hospital while Obi-Wan isn't there making his rounds.

Colchester Causeway, Lake Champlain, Vermont

Winooski River, Vermont

THE RETURN OF ERICH

Obi-Wan has transformed back into Erich the Father. Provoked, and awakened from his tranquility, he has abandoned his serene nature and decided to confront Owen.

And we thought the last couple of days on the road were going to be easy, joyful, and self-congratulatory—like the last day of the Tour de France, in which the competitors ride together arm in arm doing laps on the Champs-Élysées, sipping champagne while they ride, and goofing for the cameras.

Not quite. So much has happened in the last 36 hours, I don't even know where to start. I guess I'll just tell it in the order it happened.

First, the kids have been pushing pretty hard to get home. They are calling for big days and short rest stops. Two days ago, it was 106 miles. Today will be 95 up and over the Kancamagus Pass, in the White Mountains, then down through eastern New Hampshire to Conway, if we make it that far. (Spoiler: we didn't.) Yesterday, I hijacked our rolling convoy and directed us all down to the banks of a river in the hot afternoon. We had a splendid break swimming in the river. We swam in the cool waters, splashed around, skipped rocks, and lay on the warm boulders, staring up at the clouds drifting through the August sky.

No one said, "C'mon, time to go."

But then, after the river oasis, Owen started poking at Erich. For the past few days, he'd been variously harassing, teasing, or ridiculing his father. Yesterday, when Erich mentioned we should be thinking about where to stay for the evening (a very reasonable question, I thought), Owen started taunting him, calling him soft, ridiculing him for wanting to stop riding at a civil hour and enjoy the evening.

KANCAMAGUS PASS:

The pass, on the flank of Mt. Kancamagus near Lincoln, New Hampshire, is 2,855 feet above sea level. It is the highest point on the Kancamagus Highway (a 35-mile section of New Hampshire Route 112), affectionately known as the "Kanc." The highway is named for a high chief of the Penacook Confederacy of Native American tribes. The Kanc is one of the best fall-foliage viewing areas in the country, according to a website devoted to the highway (kancamagushighway.com), and is now designated an American Scenic Byway for "its rich history, aesthetic beauty and culture."[26]

A typical conversation between Erich and Owen looks like this:

Erich: "I know you are eager to get home, Owen, but your persistence *ad nauseam* is starting to wear thin."

Owen: "DURRRR!"

Erich: "Owen, please. Do you know what a barrel-organ litany is?"

Owen: "DURRRR! Darrel's organ! Literally!"

Erich: "A barrel organ litany is an expression that refers to monotonous and unbearable repetition. We all understand you want to get home. We also need to rest and eat."

Owen: "DURRRRR!"

The conversation went on like that, Erich patiently explaining, Owen taunting. I drifted away from them and cycled on my own. Evidently, Obi-Wan snapped. Next thing I know, he stampeded past me, with his boys in tow. If Owen wants to push on, Erich will show him what it means to push on. Erich describes that exact moment like this:

> Before we reached Montpelier, I finally broke and decided to give them exactly what they asked for. They wanted big miles, they would get big miles. I try very hard to do as I say in all things, and, in that moment, I felt that I could not back down. Because of their berating, I hated being a parent at this point, and this shitty parenting moment I am not at all proud of because I could not rise above the puerile, playground taunting of my own kids.
>
> Incidentally, I got a job offer, out of the blue, over the phone during that climb into Montpelier. They made me an offer I couldn't refuse. That was a nice tonic to soothe the emotions.

At around 7 p.m., we pull into Montpelier and take aim for an inexpensive motel. Erich pulls up short and announces, "Not us, we're pushing on for Danville."

Danville? Danville is another 30 hilly Vermont miles away. It will take them well over two hours, and the light is fading. His boys howl in protest and cry invectives at him. Erich is unflinching. We check into a motel and have a lovely dinner at a pizza place with a view of the river. It was delightful.

I receive a text message from Erich at 11:18 p.m. saying they have just stopped and are boondocking somewhere in the woods beyond Danville. So evidently, sometime after 11:00 p.m., they finally stopped and are camping in the unexamined brush outside of Danville. Good lord.

BOONDOCKING:

A term we learned back in Wyoming from a local, it means to set camp wherever you please, in woods or fields, whether permitted or not, for free.

123

Sometimes things work out for the best. Erich's flash of anger and unusual choice to push on and ride deep into the night had some lovely surprises, as he writes:

> This night ride turned out to be beautiful. The boys and I settled down after an hour, and settled in to the rhythm of the road, our turbulence absorbed by the gentle compress of evening. In the dusk we turned on lights and put on reflective vests. Dark fell, the moon rose. Silhouettes of mountains, moonlight and starlight on alpine lakes, shiny as silver coins, slid by us as we climbed into the Vermont night. We were silent, enfolded in the cadence of our breathing, our thoughts, the drone of tires rising from pavement, the cool air and dense aroma of a clear starry night, chasing, but never catching, the pools of light on the road from the bike lamps, content.

Erich's choice to separate also put us on different trajectories. Their route through Danville set him and his sons on a northern path around the White Mountains, toward Bethel, Sunday River, and then south again. We chose to ride easterly, which is a more direct, but hillier, route over the Kancamagus Highway.

We reunited last night at Panther Pond, just 25 short miles from home. We had been separated as a group for the past two days, and it was heartening to find Obi-Wan had returned, that he and his kids were back together. One of Erich's two brothers, Brady, and Brady's wife, Martha, were kind enough to host us at their lake house. Food, drinks, joy all around. The boys were out water skiing, and soon we would ride the final 25 miles to the coast to dunk our heads in the Atlantic Ocean.

The path less traveled—somewhere in Vermont

ACT YOUR WAY INTO A NEW WAY OF THINKING

The last day, Ian had the most impressive crash of the entire trip. He had his right hand in the air when Owen slowed in front of him. With only his left hand on the bars, he grabbed the front brake hard and toppled ass-over-teakettle straight across the handlebars into the road, cracking his helmet and coloring his arm and shoulder with road rash.

It was also the day that Hobbit generously buried three large, heavy rocks in my front bags. He thoughtfully let me carry those rocks all the way to my house before I discovered them.

We had a fun party that evening at our house and slept in. We spent the next day cleaning out our packs, airing out our tents, and packing Hobbit and Annie's gear to ship home. Hobbit ate a lobster roll, and we stayed up late sharing stories by the fire. The following morning, we drove Hobbit and Annie to the airport. I gave Annie the sagebrush from the Cheyenne River Reservation to keep them safe for their final passage home.

We didn't know what was going to happen on this coast-to-coast journey—we only knew we had to do it. Ultimately, most aspects of the trip turned out to be much different than we had anticipated. The landscape certainly had. On many occasions, I studied Google Maps carefully, both road and satellite images, and then conjured a picture in my head of what eastern Washington State must look like, or the Beartooth Pass, or Michigan, or the plains of South Dakota. And almost every time the landscape looked and felt much different than the image I had in my head.

The group dynamics were also different than expected. We definitely never expected the mutiny in Montana, or the emergence of Erich as Obi-Wan.

I'm reminded of a saying by the remarkable innovator and leader Jerry Sternin: "It's easier to act your way into a new way of thinking than to think your way into a new way of acting."[27]

The act of embarking on the adventure itself opened up new awareness—new ways of thinking that stretched time in unpredictable and profound ways. Each day was both eternal and timeless, yet passed in the wink of an eye. Charlie had a funny moment somewhere in Wyoming, saying, "This trip has been amazing. Life-changing. I feel totally transformed. Can I go home now?" And later, when the kids were pushing so hard at the end of the trip, we reminded them that, once we finish, the entire adventure will seem much shorter in our memory.

I recently revisited one of my favorite books, *The Top Five Regrets of the Dying.*[28] In it, Bronnie Ware, a palliative care nurse, recounts spending the final three to six weeks with dying patients and shares what they said about how they'd lived their lives, and what regrets, if any, they had.

The most common regret was, "I wish I'd had the courage to live a life true to myself, not the life others expected of me." Ware writes that most people had not honored even half of their ambitions. The choices they had made, or *not* made, had stuck with them their entire lives. It's also a reminder that our personal health brings a freedom we often don't realize until we no longer have it.

She writes that often we regret working too hard, not allowing time for escape, adventure, or renewal. She found that we also sometimes regret not having the courage to express our true feelings, or hiding them to maintain peace, which can build resentment within ourselves.

And finally, Ware writes, people often realize only later in life that happiness is a choice, which is "a surprisingly common" realization: "Many did not realize until the end that happiness is a choice. They had stayed stuck in old patterns and habits. The so-called 'comfort' of familiarity overflowed into their emotions, as well as their physical lives. Fear of change had them pretending to others, and to themselves, that they were content, when deep within, they longed to laugh properly and have silliness in their life again."

As I mentioned at the beginning of this story, most people we told about our plans before we left on this adventure said some version of "I could never do that." They would say they couldn't afford it, and yet there was Linus, whom we met at Devils Tower, cycling across the country, sleeping in cemeteries with nary a penny to his name.

They would say they didn't have the strength and stamina, and yet there was little 60-something-year-old Uli, whom we met while camping at the Mississippi River. She was cycling from Fairbanks, Alaska, to Miami, pulling a trailer with her dog in it.

They would say they don't have the time. Yet I say time is all we have. It's just up to us how we spend it.

I can tell you now, the hardest part wasn't doing it. The hardest part was getting to the starting line.

The adventure of cycling every day for two months in strange, beautiful places became part of our lifestyle. Doing it became as easy as our everyday lives. The biggest challenge was convincing ourselves and our kids to do it. Sure, there were some difficult moments on the trip, but when we were tired we rested, when we were hungry we ate, and when we were bored we played cards, jumped in the river, or went to the movies.

Life is full of unrealized dreams because we don't know how to get started. Yet it turns out the hill isn't as steep as it looks, and the trail is not as long, once we begin.

People often ask us if we think the trip was transformative in some way. I believe we don't know yet, but one thing is certain: we will never forget it. Whatever the trip means—the lessons learned, the relationships built, the strength found within ourselves, and from each other—will transform us over time.

It's been a great joy and adventure. Thanks for following along.

The Gang of Coast to Coast 2017:
Obi-Wan
Sparks
What
Hobo
Thunder
Hobbit
and myself

ACKNOWLEDGEMENTS

Writing acknowledgements is an anxious task. We're certain to leave some people out, while also looking ridiculous in attempts to name drop everyone. Well, here goes.

Once again, thank you, Pam Owen, my editor, who patiently and skillfully brought another book to life. And thank you, Jenn Bulmer for your layout expertise. It looks gorgeous. Thank you, Abbi Brockelbank for your beautiful illustrations. Thank you, my friends, Erich Bohrmann and jon holloway, for your insight and contributions to the manuscript.

We, the Coast to Coast Crew, thank our friends, new and old, we met along the journey, including Jason Rich and Jorji Knickrehm for hosting our departure, Willy Weir for the stories and inspiration, Mark Welborn for the cabin in the Cascades, Carl and his family of Richland, Washington, Tanner and his family at Waha Lake, Idaho, and thank you, Maria and Mark Rose, for shuttling us up Tom Miner Creek Road in Paradise Valley, Montana.

We thank you, Trina at the B Bar Ranch, and Larry Campbell for sharing your home near Bozeman, Montana. Thank you, Pam and Mark Myer, for bringing the beer and wigs over to Larry's house. That was silly fun. Thank you, Ben Bohrmann, for hosting us in Missoula. Thank you, Jim Sayer and the good people of AdventureCycling.org.

We thank you, Brian and Amy Weldon, for the dinner, conversation, and cornflakes, and for hosting us at your home in Chaska, Minnesota. Thanks to Jennifer and Don O'Brien for your hospitality in Whitby, Ontario. You, too, Tom Schrag, for your jokes and memories at our campsite in Minnesota, and for waking us up in the morning with donuts and coffee. Thank you, Brady and Martha Bohrmann, for sharing your home at Panther Pond in Raymond, Maine, for our final evening on the road. We appreciate that.

We thank everyone cheering and reading along as we posted blogs and photographs of the journey, notably Kath Greenhough of New Zealand, who attempted to deliver us a pizza while we were in Wyoming, but we couldn't figure out the logistics of pizza delivery while constantly moving. Thank you, Marsha Hansen, Melissa Humphries, Bob and Hannah Poe, Norm Fawcett, Peggy Hammett, Scott Brotherton, Jeff Reid, Kirsten and Scott Buchanan, Marlena Faxon and Steve Cox, Dan Edwards, Cydney and Dave Cox, Dennis Welsh and Anne Ball, Chris Strong, Gary and Laura Bergeron, Rhonda and Peter Senger, Allison Flowerdew, Chris and Celine Kuhn, Cuyler and Cindy Morris, Maura and Andrew Thornton, John Ambrose, Rachel and Mark Behrle, Edie Beattie, Ward Conant, Barbara Burnham, Robin Kynaston, Margot Cook, Kim and Luke Davidson, Molly Scholes, Rosie Cairnes down in Australia (Oi!), Maureen Moons, Rosie O'Grady, Greg and Sue Dorsey, Darlene Frederick, Martha and Jim Mackay, Darcee and Alex Pantaz, Sarah and Jeff Adams, Sean Masterman, Kevin Duffer, Dan Pontefract, Marion van Leeuwen-Kemmere, Garreth Griffith, Dawn Clegg, Kris and Susan Deal, Wendy Lamb and Matt Chappell, Keri Green, Anna Belyeav, Jeff and Jen Carr, Dede and Dave Bennell, Anton and Kim Whiley, Chris Edwards, Pam Boiros, Ricki Hagerty, Kate Zenko-Rother, Michael and Victoria Stefanakos, Pat Howe and Heidi Freeman, Danielle Saurer, Sabrina Smith, Kelly Wieber, Chris Cohen, Helen Ruisi, Gretchen and Gino Giumarro, Dana and Erik Anderson, George McDonough and Cortney Linville, Bud Roberts, Heather and Jeff Zachau, Margie Chalmers, Priti Shah, Jerry Nine, Gregorio Martinez Garrido and Ollie Ramon and family in Madrid Spain, Doug Brockelbank, Harbert Gregory, Abe and Cindy VanWingerden, Christine and Jay Mullen, Jamie and Jessica Pennington, Donna Ayer, Katherine Clark, Sharon Frain, Randall Raymond, and Kim Hallin.

Thank you, my love Amy, for holding down the fort, caring for Annie, Will, and Penny and patiently answering questions about our whereabouts. Thank you, Annie and Will, for your encouragement, and for updating the big map on the dining room table.

Thank you, Lori Andrusko Holloway, for sharing your wonderful husband for the trip.

Thank you to the Greenwood Arts Council for your constant support of the effort, and the wonderful exhibit of the trip in April 2018.

A big high-five and thank you to Sam Eubanks at Emerald City Bikes in Greenwood South Carolina, and Pete and Jamie up at Freeport Ski and Bike in Freeport, Maine. You guys are awesome and a good reminder to always support your local shop.

Thank you, Woodsie Entwistle, for your constant enthusiasm on the book project. Glad we got it done. Thank you, Dad, for the love and encouragement. I miss Mom, too.

[Note to reader: my mom, Beverly Hunter, joyfully followed the entire adventure while being treated for advanced lung cancer. She flew to Maine and greeted us when we finished on August 4, 2017. She died just a few months later on November 21, 2017.]

Most of all, thank you to my son Charlie for sharing this adventure with me. I love you.

In memory of Beverly Hunter

ENDNOTES

ABOUT THE AUTHORS

Shawn Hunter has, at various times, been a day-care wrangler in Colorado, a teacher in Korea, a plucky entrepreneur, and a best-selling author of books that are completely unlike this one. Through his writing, he would like you to think he is an adventurous swashbuckler of a man, daring and clever. But in reality, he spends most days terrified of his daughter's bunny rabbit, planning the next family meal, and pondering what to do about his growing number of incomplete projects. He lives with his far-more-competent and beautiful wife, Amy, and their three children, in Maine.

jon o. holloway is a true Sagittarius who loves the call of the open road. At the age of nine, he turned a cave into a darkroom and processed his first roll of film. He now shares the beauty and community of the world through photography. He earned his MFA from the Savannah College of Art and Design and teaches at Lander University. He lives on a farm in South Carolina comprising 10,000 trees, two creeks, three dogs, two fish, two horses, nine hens, two cats, one kid named Annie, and a beautiful wife.